FROM THE BARE STEM

FROM THE BARE STEM

Making Dorothy Elmhirst's

GARDEN
at
DARTINGTON HALL

REGINALD SNELL

DEVON BOOKS
IN ASSOCIATION WITH
THE DARTINGTON PRESS

First published in Great Britain in 1989
by Devon Books

Designed by Sue Snell for Scriveners
Typesetting by P&M Typesetting Ltd

ISBN: 0 86114–849–5

British Library Cataloguing-in-Publication Data

Snell, Reginald
From the Bare Stem: Making Dorothy Elmhirst's Garden at Dartington Hall.
1. England, Country houses. Gardens. Design I. Title
712'.6'0942

DEVON BOOKS

Official Publisher to Devon County Council
An imprint of Wheaton Publishers Ltd.
A Member of Maxwell Pergamon Publishing Corporation plc

Wheaton Publishers Ltd
Hennock Road, Marsh Barton, Exeter,
Devon EX2 8RP
Tel: 0392 74121;
Telex 42794 (WHEATN G)

Printed and bound in Great Britain by
A. Wheaton & Co Ltd

In Memory

DOROTHY ELMHIRST

1887–1968

ACKNOWLEDGEMENTS

I am grateful to a number of people, among them Maurice Ash, Peter Cox, Pom Elmhirst, Michael Harley, Robert Hening, Robin Johnson, John Lane, Paula Morel, Kevin Mount, Mary Bride Nicholson, Willi Soukop and Terry Underhill, for help and advice. I want in particular to thank two others: in writing about the contents of the garden I have been both informed and guided by Mary Bartlett, and in setting out the chronological sequence of events I have depended on Dartington's historian Victor Bonham-Carter, who generously told me I might quarry as I would in his masterly unpublished *Report to the Trustees* – there are whole sections of the narrative where my part has been that of a child with his box of crayons, colouring for pleasure a picture that was already accurately drawn.

R.S.

CONTENTS

FOREWORD

For the preservation of the Dartington garden we must all be truly thankful. Indeed for its existence at all. For it is one of the last great gardens to be made in Britain – great in its area and its conception, but also in the inspiration that went into its creation.

Today it may be simple to move mountains of earth, to raise hills and lower valleys, to make lakes and plant woodland all by machinery, not by shovel, barrow and wagon. But once the plan of a garden has been realized on the ground it needs maintaining. Machines cannot supplant every skilled touch, nor computers replace the judgement that comes with years of looking at natural things. Even public authorities administering large reserves of cash cannot contemplate the expense of looking after a new garden as expansive as Dartington's. Multi-national companies are known to plant parks round their offices, but always they specify low maintenance, and they are more pre-occupied with concealing car parks and enhancing their prestige than expressing the kind of sympathies that lay behind the making of Dartington.

Dorothy Elmhirst may have enjoyed great wealth and lived at a time when this could still be used to achieve almost any whim, great or small, but she also had vision and an unflagging love of everything that grows upon the earth. The garden she made has grandeur but it is also an intimate garden where you feel someone has ordered this or that for her own quiet delight and is anxious to share this with others. That is why I speak of it in the singular rather than use the more impersonal plural.

Although Dartington garden belongs to its time it is timeless in the way that a work of art retains a freshness through centuries. The horticultural fashions it embraces have become part of the mainstream of garden development. It is a successful amalgam of several styles; its free-standing trees reflect the traditional English parkland, its vistas cleverly exploit natural features, and its dense shrub and ground cover plantings are a large-scale essay in woodland gardening. The interplay of turf and shrubs looks forward to the art of the landscapist of today, and heathers employ the palette of the colour-conscious garden-maker forced by necessity to make saving in labour a priority. Landscaping and garden-making are twin arts that too often go separate ways: Dartington marries the two in a successful and enduring partnership.

Never would I drive down the A38 without watching for the Totnes signpost and turning off south here. Excitement mounts as the names on the lesser signposts slip past. When Staverton appears and that narrow bridge is passed, soon to be followed by a glimpse of the church tower rising above the trees, a very important moment is at hand. Left again, up the winding hill, quickly out of the car park and through the great wooden doors and I am back in a garden I have learned to love as much as any, and much more than most of those where I am a frequent visitor. However often I go back, Dartington never loses its magic, never fails to reveal something fresh.

Always I pause at the sight of the Courtyard and the fresh green of the swamp cypress tree just there to the right. Ahead is the matchless backdrop of the Great Hall, and lying in front like a stylish carpet of welcome is that ingeniously designed path, a little hard to the tread, but one in which stone has been so artfully used. I look round to the right to assure myself that the cascading holboellia climber has survived yet another winter and I hope this is a moment when I shall catch it in scented flower. I look along to the east-facing border which the buildings, so prettily patterned with their windows and their little projecting gables, shelter. Is the Tasmanian billardiera carrying its lustrous blue fruits? And I go from one silvery Mediterranean shrub to the other, all planted to merge with the colour of the stone and all of them a reminder that this is a garden where full advantage has been taken of a gentle climate and where the original planters were endlessly resourceful.

Taking a respectful look at the camellias on the wall of the Buttery, I go towards that well-proportioned lead urn that has never been moved from its pedestal through all the years I have been coming here. An abrupt turn right and down the steps and the Tiltyard, the Sunny Border and the whole panorama of the rhododendron and camellia plantings, those mighty chestnuts, the sobering set of Irish yews, come into view.

But there are many details to explore yet. I look to see what has been added or lost by chill against the bastion-like retaining wall behind the Sunny Border. I lament of course the loss of the great *Cornus capitata*, but I note the new inches put on by its young successor. I note, too, the progress made by the old

Japanese maples with lace-like foliage. Always I have difficulty in deciding whether to take the Rhododendron Walk or the Camellia Walk first and end up by covering both, retracing my steps as I look for the cyclamen and peer into the woodland floor to assure myself the hellebores are self-sowing. Then on to Higher Meadow with a special look to see if the stuartia trees are in flower or have budded successfully this season.

So I come out to the Memorial Pavilion and stand once more at the head of that descending glade, a viewpoint from which one can see how successfully the prospect of the countryside beyond has been brought into this varied but tranquil garden. Even the puff of smoke and the distant whistle of the train that takes a winding course close to the river down there in the valley seem part of it.

All this – the trees and the turf, the splendour and the incidents, the open glades, the vistas and the hedges, the serene and the exciting moments – all this, encountered by those who come to Dartington for study, refreshment or inspiration, perhaps all three, and, changed by it, always take away something of it which they will keep for ever, means so much to me that I am overwhelmingly delighted that at last Dartington's garden is being celebrated as it should be in a book of its own, a monograph that recounts the history and pays respect to all who made it and the influences that played upon them, influences that now rebound and touch all who visit it. Yes, this book will be bought as a souvenir, but it is also an evocation, a wide screen overall view of one of the great episodes in the history of twentieth century garden-making, so richly appropriate to the whole Dartington venture.

Fred Whitsey

CHAPTER I

THE SETTING

It is an old story: a traveller comes home after an absence of nineteen years and discovers his father alone in the vineyard hoeing round a plant. The old man's head is bowed; he is wearing a filthy, tattered coat, leather gaiters and gloves to protect his hands against the thorns. At first he does not realize who is watching him and he is bewildered by what the stranger seems to know – until he declares: "I can tell you all the trees you gave me one day on this garden terrace. I was only a little boy at the time, trotting after you through the orchard, begging you for this and that, and as we wound our way among the trees you told me all their names. You gave me thirteen pear trees and ten apple trees and forty fig trees, and you pointed out the fifty rows of vines that were to be my very own." In the end, of course, Laertes knows it must be his son, Odysseus, returned – and how can a Recognition Scene ever fail?

Many a father since that day has thought it his duty to do a bit of work in the garden before the light begins to fade, glad enough to be accompanied by his small son, wishing perhaps that the boy wouldn't talk quite so much. Odysseus grew to manhood – and went on talking to the very end, often with good effect. Laertes was doubtless glad to have him back – for a while – but he was soon out in the garden again with his hoe, since the weeds were gaining on him.

From earliest times the Garden has been the very stuff of mythology. Once it was ours, "to dress it and to keep it", and banishment from the Garden was the beginning of all our woes. It is the key to many of our most precious childhood memories; it is a symbol of the unending search for that simplicity of living which we should never have abandoned, and might yet recover if we would, not in some distant country but close at home. The making of a garden – any garden – is one of the oldest and most rewarding of the arts, and its tending is the most ordinary, the most universal of human pursuits. Civilization itself could almost be described as a condition of human society where stories are told and gardens made. The story that follows is a way of remembering one human being by describing the making of one such garden.

The scene is a partly ruined medieval manor house, standing within a wide bend of the river Dart in South Devon, two miles upstream from the ancient Saxon burgh of Totnes. Begun in Richard II's reign, between 1388 and 1399, and built for the king's half-brother John Holand, Dartington Hall is the only existing house of its period in the country, and has one of the largest residential courtyards surviving from the entire Middle Ages. Its early military associations came to an end in the middle of the sixteenth century, and the house was lived in by eleven generations of a single Devon family, the Champernownes, who managed the property for nearly four hundred years. During the nineteenth century it became impossible for them to keep it in good repair and in 1925 the whole estate was put up for sale. The purchasers were Leonard and Dorothy Elmhirst, both then in their thirties, and it was to become not only their first married home but the centre of a wide-ranging and radically new social experiment.

The garden lies close to the medieval house, and house and garden form only a small part of a thousand-acre estate, mostly woodland and farming country. The immediate surroundings of the Hall and courtyard form a kind of island, bounded for most of the way by a road, and to a lesser extent by farm land. This is the true 'heart' of Dartington – and, curiously, it has the traditional shape of a heart, the cleft being the site of the look-out near Henry Moore's Reclining Figure, and the bottom point touching the curve of the road by the Round House near the entrance archway. The whole 'heartland' measures 28 acres. Some of it is clearly not landscape garden – for instance the kitchen garden, the church tower and graveyard, the courtyard buildings, the Garden Centre and greenhouses, and the buildings which are used by the Dartington College of Arts. The size of the garden proper – that is to say all the area covered by grass, paving, flower beds, shrubbery or woodland – amounts to 21¼ acres, almost exactly three quarters of the whole. Though Nymans in Sussex and Hever Castle in Kent are somewhat larger (each has thirty acres), other comparable modern gardens are somewhat smaller: Pyrford Court in Surrey (twenty acres), Hidcot in the Cotswolds and Sissinghurst in Kent (nine acres), Great Dixter in Sussex (three and a half acres) and Tintinhull in Somerset (three quarters of an acre).

The central feature of the garden, to which all other areas are necessarily related, is a wide, flat lawn flanked by a series of grass terraces, that is always

The seeds of Leonard Elmhirst's plans for Dartington were sown when he journeyed to India during the First World War. The experience led him to take a course in agriculture at Cornell University, where he met Dorothy Whitney Straight, widow of the American financier Willard Straight and daughter of the statesman and businessman William C Whitney. Dorothy decided to back Leonard when she heard of his plan to return to India to join the Indian author and philosopher Rabindranath Tagore in West Bengal. There he spent three and a half years creating an Institute for Rural Reconstruction before handing it over in 1923 to Indian staff. He and Dorothy were married in April 1925; six months later, after spending their honeymoon on a private yacht in the Caribbean, they bought Dartington Hall.

referred to as the Tiltyard – and there is very good historical evidence that it was originally used as such in the early part of the fifteenth century. It is generally supposed that the whole of this area, together with the terraces that bound three sides of it, was coeval with John Holand's manor house and hall; but whether the whole terrain could be called a medieval garden is more doubtful. Nearer to London, it is true, noblemen's gardens were being cultivated, but it would be a mistake to picture these as looking in any way 'olde Englysshe': they were more probably ordered and formal in the continental tradition – European gardens off the coast of Europe, in fact. The true English Garden, as we now conceive it, had yet to be invented. In any case, Holand was a soldier, living a long way from London, and the inventory of his belongings, made after his downfall, contains much mention of weapons of war and jousting but none of garden implements. In the course of time gardens of some sort must have been made, but they are not chronicled. Facts are few, but a story survives – it is no more – that Sir Walter Raleigh once produced plans for a water garden at Dartington, at the request of his uncle Admiral Champernowne.

Throughout the nineteenth century, then, there was a garden of some kind at Dartington, both for ornament and for use. But during the early part of our own century it became increasingly neglected, particularly during the years that followed the 1914–18 war. When Leonard and Dorothy Elmhirst bought the estate in 1925 the kitchen gardens were managed by a tenant, and the shrubs, lawns and flower beds in the private garden had been largely untended. The Champernownes themselves, whose family had managed the estate since the first year of Queen Elizabeth's reign, had found the increasingly dilapidated private house no longer habitable with any degree of comfort, and had moved out four years previously. The scene outside was one of near-total dereliction: the last of the family's gardeners had left his employment not long before, and the Elmhirsts were glad of permission to staff the gardens even before negotiations for the purchase of the estate were completed. This was not much more than a 'holding operation': generally speaking, the garden staff did not exceed half a dozen throughout the next three years.

When Leonard described his first impressions of the estate, in a letter written in March 1925 to Dorothy in the United States, he did not refer to the garden in any detail – "the garden and trees you must see for yourself" was all that he said – and it was to the total magic of the place, not to any particular feature, that he had surrendered so completely on that winter's day. It had clearly been an overwhelming experience for him: "a thousand visions surge into my mind at the thought of you and the possibilities of our adventure together in Devonshire, – it grows more thrilling every moment, and I can hardly contain myself . . . We ran down to the valley of the Dart to find Dartington Hall, but we couldn't find an entrance. Finally we crept along a little cutting and came to a thatched lodge and gate with a bridge over a bubbling brooklet – in we went and up and down some wonderful hills till we pulled up in a veritable fairy land – in winter too – what it would be like in spring or summer or autumn I dare not imagine. I wanted to kneel and worship the beauty of it all." Thereafter there is nothing on paper to show how their thinking went, and we have no means of knowing when they began seriously to consider what was, after all, only one of an enormous number of projects that went to form the 'English experiment', as they called it. Many of these needed immediate attention, but the garden could afford to wait for a while.

The nature of their plan for Dartington amounted to nothing less than the furtherance of the Good Society – of happy, responsible, creative living – through education, the study and practice of the arts and the development of new methods of farming and industry on a sound economic basis, in a decaying rural area. Leonard Elmhirst had a particular concern for forestry, farm management and the practical needs of agricultural workers. Dorothy believed passionately in the arts as a means of personal and communal enrichment. Both had a keen social conscience, and shared many of the same qualities: vision, courage, flexibility, the willingness to reach out beyond conventional thinking and practice in pursuit of a full life that was to be fully shared with their fellows.

Much – some have thought far too much – that was done at Dartington during those early years of the 'experiment' was not thought out, but simply allowed to happen. Leonard instinctively rejected creeds and tidy categories; he generally preferred to support developments that seemed to have their own inner momentum – he was, in the best sense, an opportunist, but it was often inspired opportunism. There are important features in the Dartington of today that were no part of his original plan, yet he encouraged their growth: his indication was always to follow 'the way the sap was flowing'. It is difficult, at this distance in time, to avoid the impression that the garden was an exception to this tendency, and easy to suppose that its making was the most completely planned of all the undertakings at Dartington. It certainly looks as if Dorothy was at last realizing a long cherished 'garden dream'. But much that she later said and wrote strongly suggests that this is a misapprehension. Clearly, it always occupied a more central place in her thoughts than in his, and their friends used to recall that, while she spoke of "our garden", he would normally refer to it – courteously, but realistically – as "your garden". They were united about what they wanted to make, but its maintenance once made was in a real sense her own personal concern.

Neither of them had much previous experience of gardening, though Leonard was brought up in the country and, when he married Dorothy, had just completed in two years a four years' diploma course in agriculture in the United States. His parental home at Laxton in Yorkshire, where his father was curate, was not far from the 1,300-acre estate at Elmhirst which had been lived in by members of the family since the thirteenth century. Like his five brothers, Leonard had as a child been allocated a piece of ground, which his parents persuaded – almost ordered – him to plant with pansies and the like, and keep properly weeded. As the eldest son he was always the leader in outdoor activities: it was he who constructed a rockery, and he was by general fraternal consent in charge of it, even as late as his mid-twenties. The children had the run of a traditional walled garden, such as had been known to his forebears for the past five generations at least, and their playground included a small greenhouse and that mysterious shed where the gardener kept all his tools and equipment, with a space for pots and a bench for potting and seeding.

Dorothy's upbringing had been urban: her childhood home was "a very beautiful house in New York, a kind of Renaissance palace" built by her father, where the walls were hung with Gobelin tapestries and paintings by Raphael, Rubens and Van Dyck, and the Sunday evening music recital might be given by Fritz Kreisler. She came, during her later years, to love gardens deeply, almost obsessively, but she had to wait until she was forty before she found herself – with increasing confidence and increasing delight – in charge of a garden of her own.

CHAPTER II

"THE ESSENTIAL FORM"

The trees were a priceless inheritance, and, though increasingly vulnerable, remain so today. Many of the finest date from the nineteenth century – several oaks, beeches, London planes, Scots pines, the Monterey pine on one of the lower terraces, and the swamp cypress in the Courtyard near the entrance archway. There is indeed one group which pre-dates all of these: the oldest of the great Spanish chestnuts on the upper terrace belong at the very latest to the mid-sixteenth century – planted, therefore, by the first Champernownes who acquired the property in 1559 – but they are considered by some to be well over five hundred years old, and thus contemporary with the Hall itself. A few of those on the tiltyard terrace have undergone extensive tree surgery – some of it unusually bold for the 1920s – in order to prolong their life, but in spite of their great age they still bear a good crop of nuts. Of the other trees

From the beginning Dorothy Elmhirst recognized that the garden landscape had great possibilities and that her first task must be to lay bare the underlying structure by clearing away the non-essentials. "The area had three outstanding gifts", she was to write many years later. "First, the natural contours of the land, the shapes, the essential form that lay underneath everything else – how could we intensify these shapes and make them count? Then the trees; thank heaven they were there, but you couldn't really see most of them. How could we uncover those great trunks and show them off in their great nobility and beauty? Lastly, the discovery and embellishment of architectural and historical features. Some we had to uncover, some to release, some to reveal and some to emphasize. The spectators' terraces were there, but we found that the tiltyard itself had been cut in two, excavated at the lower end to make a pit for bull and bear baiting with dogs. Hence in all probability the Twelve Apostles were put in to conceal the brutalities from the nursery windows. At the top end the earth had been piled up to form a rose garden with box edging."

In the early summer of 1925 Percy Woods became the first of a line of long-serving Head Gardeners at Dartington – his four successors span well over half a century between them. Woods was given the job of clearing and restoring the private garden to something like its earlier condition and general appearance during the nineteenth century.

He and his men began work on the grass that had grown completely out of hand on the lawn nearest the Hall and the Bowling Green further to the South; this was cut in the later stages by a small hand-pushed mowing machine, but before that by scythe. Their next jobs were the clearing of brambles and creepers from the main Courtyard buildings, to make possible a proper inspection of the structure, and the removal of the walls that subdivided the Courtyard itself, separating the still fairly presentable private lawn at the Hall end from the other section at the entrance end, which was no more than an

mentioned above, the magnificent Holm oak may well date from before 1800. Its neighbour the Lucombe oak, of a variety mostly seen in Devon, is likely to be an original planting of its time, when the Exeter nurseryman was raising the first specimens towards the end of the eighteenth century. The fine London planes, standing at the end of the terraces near the Dell, are probably a century and a half old. The Monterey pine, a native of California, could be one of the first to reach this country when PINUS-RADIATA was introduced early in the last century. The twelve clipped Irish yews, right, must also be dated not long after 1800; they are, like all their kind, descended from a single parent tree found in County Fermanagh, and are sometimes known as Florence Court yews. A special treasure that was brought to Dartington in 1915 was the 'Handkerchief Tree' (DAVIDIA INVOLUCRATA), above, a native of China now to be found near the Swans fountain. The present specimen has grown up from the base of its magnificent predecessor, one of the first and finest to be found anywhere in this country, which was brought down by a freak snowstorm in 1969.

unusually untidy farmyard. Proper repair of the Hall was planned to begin much later, but immediately there was a large box tree to be removed – from inside the building, which had been roofless for the past hundred years. In the gardens beyond, the months that followed saw much shifting of flower beds and banks of earth that had piled up against the front of the private house, the removal of a deep belt of 20ft-high laurels near the kitchen gardens, and the clearing of a tangle of brambles, laurels and rhododendrons that had been allowed to grow rampant between the upper entrance drive and the Tiltyard.

New flower beds were being dug as old ones were removed; vigorous pruning was undertaken, shrubs and trees were cut down, and the rabbits reduced in number. At one point an old cider press was discovered in the undergrowth, and moved to the centre of a square lawn in the Dutch garden that earlier Champernownes had made at the upper end of the Tiltyard. At its lower end there had evidently once been a formal rose garden, only slightly below the level of the Twelve Apostles, but this had been filled in, and was now a tangle of rubbish, brambles and shrubbery, little more than a large and unsightly hole. At this stage, too, the old entrance drive was closed as such and became what it is now, the lowest of a series of parallel paths across the head of the valley. Originally it had continued, after reaching the front door of the private house, along the whole of what is always called the south front of the house and the Hall (though in fact these buildings face almost due south-west), skirting the corner of the kitchen and keeping close to the lower Courtyard range, to join the road down to Totnes. From now on there was to be no wheeled traffic moving inside the gardens, other than garden machinery and visitors' cars which drove in by the wrong entrance.

By 1928, at the end of three years' unremitting labour – which had really amounted to little else than preparing the ground – it had become clear to the Elmhirsts that expert help from outside would be needed. Woods and his staff had brought the whole area to a state where work might be begun, but its overall design was beyond their powers. Thus, during the next forty years, advice was sought from three outside consultants, H. Avray Tipping, Beatrix Farrand and Percy Cane.

Harry Tipping, then in his early seventies, was an unusually versatile man. As an Oxford undergraduate in the late 1870s he had been a colourful member of the 'greenery-yallery' aesthetic scene, and later always retained a certain eccentricity of voice and manner. On the testimony of those who knew him well he was "a very fine actor", "an excellent cook", and "knew more about political economy than anyone in England", which suggests at least that he had good friends. He was a connoisseur of architecture, wood-carving, furniture, silver and china, and a copious contributor to the *Dictionary of National Biography*; he made a special study of building craftmanship, was the author of the standard work on Grinling Gibbons, and – beginning in his early fifties – became a successful journalist, writing for *Country Life* a series of articles on great houses which were later collected to form his massive eight-volume set of *English Homes*. In addition, he was for more than seventy years a practising gardener and garden designer. Altogether he seemed a fairly safe choice for Dartington: he had been an eager disciple of William Robinson and Gertrude Jekyll in their campaign for 'natural planting', and was clearly no extremist. He was known to believe in a mixture of the calculated and the unconstrained, and his normal practice was to compose a formal design in immediate relation to a house, which was then merged into the naturalism of woodland – and, where possible, water – further off. The overall aim was thus a kind of 'sweet disorder in the dress' that was itself most carefully cut and sewn. The Elmhirsts wanted to learn from Tipping whether it might be possible to develop the garden both as an amenity and at the same time as a commercial venture – one obvious implication of the 'Dartington experiment'. They had already realized that the neighbourhood enjoyed a climate peculiarly favourable to horticulture. It was, for instance, possible to grow there a number of plants that did not prosper further east, and indeed almost as many sub-tropical plants as in parts of Cornwall. And they wanted to know what the prospects were of meeting part of the overheads of a country house garden from the profits of a commercial gardening business.

Their exchange of letters was followed by an extended period in which nothing appeared to be happening: it looked, indeed, as if Tipping was playing 'hard to get', for he kept postponing his suggested visit. Early in 1927 he finally came, he saw, and believed he would conquer the problems put to him. He soon produced an overall plan, and suggested working in harness with William Weir, whom Leonard had recently invited to be in sole charge of the medieval fabric at Dartington. Tipping was an admirer of Weir's work, and had, in successive contributions to *English Homes*, already written with enthusiasm and understanding of his achievements at Penshurst Place, Oakham Castle and Tattershall. Tipping, who had begun by 'dragging his feet', now seemed to Leonard to be hurrying too much – he had just written to ask if his plans for autumn and winter work were being carried out, but Leonard was disinclined to take orders from him. The following revealing letter, which Leonard sent to Weir, suggests that there were times when simply too much was happening at Dartington for anyone's comfort: (12 August 1927) "Mr Tipping has suggested coming again – could you connect up with him and pay us a visit about the same time? I am afraid he may be very disappointed at our not having done anything this summer to the garden, but it is quite impossible to do everything at once; and, as you know, with a gang of 200 men on construction work of one kind or another, with a school into the bargain, it has not been easy to find the time and the leisure which are essential if one is to take the right kind of interest in garden reconstruction... I have insisted from the start that the bread and butter end of this experiment must come first, and that we are not an ordinary country house for entertainment. We have therefore sacrificed the ornamental garden this time for the production end. This does not mean that I do not value the former, but that the following out of Mr Tipping's plan cannot always be carried through immediately."

It sounds a little as if Leonard was looking around for an ally; in that case, the choice of Weir was odd – he was, and always remained, on formal terms with this Scotsman whom he later described as "a man of few words". Certainly the notion of this silent church repairer as an 'agony uncle' is not an easy one to entertain; but the two men did in fact visit Dartington for a shared working week-end, and were jointly responsible for the loggia that stands close to the front door of the private house – though for nothing more thereafter.

Tipping submitted his final plan early in 1928, and its results can be seen today. Almost all his work at Dartington concerns the area that lies between, and links, the 'lived in' part of the estate and the garden proper. This is clearly needed to preserve some kind of privacy, as being an extension of the house itself, easily accessible from indoors without any sense of crossing a boundary; it must yet remain closely related to the other great features of the the garden that lay behind it, where in fact Tipping did little but renovate the flat surfaces of the tiltyard terraces and make a start on the Heath Garden. Nearer the house, he used yew planting to good effect: he planned the hedge at the eastern end of the Bowling Green, and the second hedge that runs up to the corner of the Old Kitchen – between them they enclose all the private area of the garden that lies closest to the house, separating it firmly from the Great Lawn and the entrance drive.

His work also included the construction of another important feature of the garden's lay-out: the full acceptance of its ruined masonry as part of the landscape. The arches (as they appear to be) that stand on the South Lawn, and are sometimes referred to as the Arcade [see page 21], are in fact neither: they are window heads whose lower portion has been blocked up by the shifting of ground levels in previous centuries, and are probably all that survives of a Long Gallery, of uncertain date, that gave spectators a clear view of the tiltyard below. Tipping built a retaining wall on either side of the 'arches', and the low

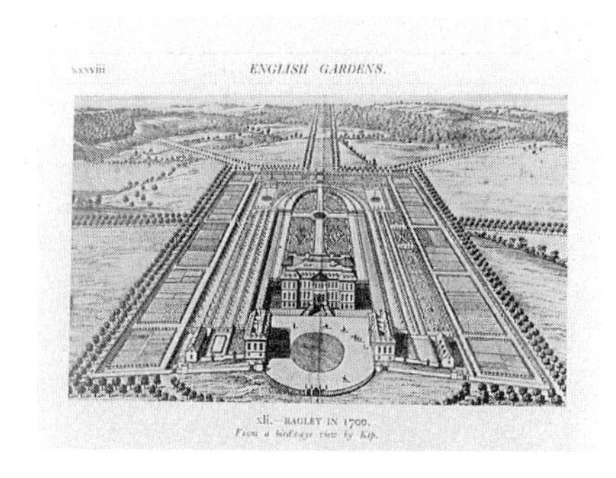
xxxviii ENGLISH GARDENS.

xli.—RAGLEY IN 1700.
From a bird's-eye view by Kip.

A page from another of Harry Tipping's COUNTRY LIFE *publications,* ENGLISH GARDENS.

William Weir, here photographed in his mid-twenties, was a pupil and associate of Philip Webb and William Morris. By the time he came to Dartington his reputation as the most accomplished conservation architect of his generation was secure, although, remarkably, his career had another quarter century to run. Born at the high noon of Victorianism and still working in his eighties as a church repairer for the Society for the Protection of Ancient Buildings, he lived until 1950.

wall that now runs the full length of the Bowling Green, just above the Tiltyard, thus establishing the beginnings of the long herbaceous border, one of the garden's most attractive features, which, because of her particular and personal work there, became known as 'Dorothy's Sunny Border'.

Hardly more than two years after the first of his only two visits to Dartington, Tipping wrote to Leonard Elmhirst: (7 August 1929) "I rather gather that the plans I made for abolishing the drive and laying out loggia, terraces etc are not being carried out and that what you now intend there is planned to your liking. I think, therefore, the moment has come when it may be said that my professional connection with the work at Dartington can be considered closed." Leonard too thought that it could be so considered, and Harry Tipping made no further visits. But Dartington and its first consultant remained on friendly terms, and if this episode had perhaps not been all that Leonard and Dorothy had hoped, Tipping had made a significant contribution to the garden plan; more important, he had recommended a worthy successor: through the good offices of the Director of Kew Gardens, a friend of his, he had found in Stewart Lynch a gardener who served Dartington for the next fifteen years. "I have seen Lynch", he wrote to Leonard in November 1928; "we had a long talk on Dartington, and I feel certain that the garden there is safe in his hands."

In the autumn of 1928 Lynch was made Garden Superintendent (this was the first use of the title at Dartington), and continued in this and other capacities until his final retirement in 1943. His gardening credentials were impressive: he had been trained as a boy by his father Richard Lynch, Curator of the Cambridge University Botanic Gardens and the man who established these as second in importance to Kew among English public gardens. After appointments at Lyon and Versailles, and work as a student gardener with the Rothschild family near Cannes, he returned to England, enlisted in the Army, and after the end of the Great War did two years' service with the Imperial War Graves Commission.

Lynch's early years in the Dartington gardens saw a considerable increase in the size of the staff, and the introduction – largely due to his recommendations – of a radical division of outdoor activities on the Estate. Nursery, kitchen gardens, glass houses and community garden were now managed as separate undertakings, and there was even the possibility of a scientific garden, since Lynch wanted at one time to make Dartington a showplace for rare botanical specimens. Dorothy herself was from the start, and would remain, particularly concerned with the Garden as Art, but other parallel – and very successful – developments such as the Garden as Commerce and the Garden as Education should not be forgotten, since they were all integral to the 'experiment'.

One of Stewart Lynch's early tasks was the completion of the Sunny Border and the making of a stone-paved path beside it, originally only four feet wide but later much extended. The lawns, beds and terraces above the tennis courts were finished, the Bowling Green was renovated and the yew hedges advocated by Harry Tipping were planted. There was much clearance of undergrowth, and the grass terraces that surround the tiltyard area were renewed. Lynch was also responsible for the construction of a children's playground, for work in the Courtyard to be described later, for the creation of a heath garden on the steep ground below the present site of Henry Moore's sculpture, and the making of a water garden higher up the valley.

The Open Air Theatre in the mid-1930s.

The construction of the Open Air Theatre – perhaps his most important project at Dartington – occupied Lynch for two full years. When the central area was first cleared, its lower part, the Sunken Garden below the Twelve Apostles, was planted with azaleas, rhododendrons and a large monkey puzzle tree (heartily disliked by Leonard and felled by him and his brothers Victor, Richard and Pom). The higher part was the formal Dutch garden made by the Champernownes, with the old cider press as its centrepiece. This whole lay-out was now completely altered. The cider press was moved to a new position higher up, near the water garden, and the Sunken Garden was raised by the shifting of earth from the higher part. A slightly raised stage was formed at the lower end of the Tiltyard, the whole area was grass-sown, and rows of young yews were planted to form in time both the 'backcloth' and the 'wings' on either side of the acting area. The auditorium consisted of a series of shallow lawns, flanked by the original grass-sown terraces, which were now more clearly defined and gradually renewed. One of Leonard Elmhirst's early Dartington snapshots shows a series of gently undulating slopes, and is accompanied by a hand-written note that reads: "Terraces probably untouched since 14th century. Mr Lynch 'did them up'." Lynch not only superintended the work but was himself responsible for the plan of the theatre.

Special attention was given at this time to the Twelve Apostles, which were much overgrown: two men working inside the trees cut out all the dead wood, pruned the tops back into an even line and attached wire ties to hold the branches into a symmetrical shape. Lynch was, in addition to all this, responsible for planting a wide variety of shrubs in many areas of the garden.

CHAPTER III

THE ENGLISH GARDEN

In their early years at Dartington it might have appeared that the Elmhirsts were consciously planning and working within a definite gardening tradition; yet it is hard to reconcile their evident sure-footedness with their comparative lack of theoretical knowledge and practical experience, and hard to suppose that they realized, except gradually and fitfully, what traditions they were following. Two things are clear: first, that during the early years at Dartington they were mainly concerned to make a garden that would be worthy of the splendid buildings they had acquired – no more than that, though that was much; secondly, that ten years later they were wholly committed to the idea of a particular kind of garden, whose style and character cannot have been in Leonard's mind when he first broke through the undergrowth that lay beyond the ruins of the Old Kitchen. The style was wholly traditional, and the character wholly English – seemingly a double paradox, since many of their beliefs and practices were boldly radical, and there was little in Dorothy that could be called English. Yet both had strong traditional roots, Leonard notably in his historical interest, and Dorothy perhaps in her artistic and religious disposition. Although she was herself an American, and was soon to enlist the help of a fellow-countrywoman in the planning of the garden, all ideas of 'foreign' influence in the grounds of Dartington are, as we shall see, quite misplaced.

It is not entirely clear whether Dorothy 'found' the English garden through the teachings of her second consultant Beatrix Farrand, or whether she sought Mrs Farrand's help because she had already made her own discovery and needed only to have it confirmed. But there is at least no question that, whatever it may have looked like at the time, her initial approach to garden making had been very tentative: many years later she confessed that "here at Dartington we have never been able to visualize the whole design from the start, following a plan made on paper. We worked step by step, doing practical

The title page from PARADISI IN SOLE PARADISUS *(literally "Park-in-Sun's Earthly Paradise") by John Parkinson, published in 1629.*

jobs first, and only gradually came to realize the important features of the place." The recognition of what she was looking for – one of the most important Recognition Scenes of her life – was slow in coming, but when it came it brought an overwhelming certainty that never thereafter deserted her. Later in life she often referred to her discovery of the English garden, and she spelt it out most clearly in a talk that she gave – it is undated, but probably belongs to her late sixties – beginning with these words: "I would like to trace with you tonight the origin and development of the English garden – is there something we can call 'the English garden'?" The material for the rest of the talk is in the form of notes, but its emphasis was mainly on the work of William Robinson with his advocacy of the 'natural', and that of Gertrude Jekyll with her painterly approach to garden making – Dorothy once described Miss Jekyll delightfully as "a horticultural Impressionist". She speaks respectfully enough of the great masters of formalism, who treated the garden as only one aspect of architectural design, and her head does not underrate their importance; but her heart is elsewhere. She quotes with evident approval the saying of eighteenth century William Kent that "Nature abhors a straight line", but declares that he and his contemporaries, though they may have been diligently seeking it, never actually entered the inmost shrine: "18th century gardens belonged to painted Nature, 19th century ones to Nature herself". And there is no mistaking the warmth of her concluding words: "Throughout all these changes of style, cottage gardens have remained, full of flowers and scent and fresh loveliness".

There has long been an English tradition of what is 'natural' in a garden. Certain similarities suggest themselves here with the development of our language, which has – far beyond all others – always been prepared to accept, adapt and absorb words from many parts of the world. Very large numbers of these have so quickly, and so completely, become naturalized that we are quite unaware of their origin. But the analogy can be pushed too far: really to feel at home in a garden, the Englishman likes to be reminded of something he knows well – that recalls, perhaps, his own childhood. He will give an occasional courteous welcome to a foreign import, but he never entirely forgets that it is 'from abroad'. Exotic linguistic growths he will often make wholly his own, exotic horticultural ones not nearly so often. In the seventeenth century, it is true, our forefathers fully accepted a few oriental influences, which have since become fused with the native tradition, and continental practices clearly flourished in Tudor times. But the absorption was not total: Hampton Court was certainly formal, but still unmistakably English, not Italianate; the paths were laid out in orderly fashion, but rose trees were everywhere rampant. The geometric knot garden, though long fashionable, was 'unnatural' to many English eyes.

The authentic 'feel' of Englishness, when continental and native traditions seem finally to have been merged, and regularity of form and a certain wildness of character were finally reconciled, had a long time to wait. During the eighteenth century the whole appearance of this country was transformed by gardeners, so that now large areas of rural England are man-made landscapes. The great 'improvers', such as William Kent, Lancelot Brown and Humphry Repton, were really only doing on a vast scale what many a country dweller was seeking to do in the small patch of open ground that surrounded his home. In essence, many of our grandest gardens are only cottage gardens writ large.

The changes that gardening, both large and small-scale, underwent during this period represent a genuinely national revolution in taste and practice, and they were profoundly influenced – as is the English way of allowing the several arts, even art and morality, to overlap one another – by writers, painters and philosophers. Alexander Pope, one of the real pioneers of modern garden design, worked for twenty five years on his garden at Twickenham in search of the Picturesque. Here was the parallel with the later literary Romantic movement. Nature was for Pope "At once the source and end and test of Art". Gertrude Jekyll, herself trained as a painter, consciously applied the colour theories of Goethe to the creation of harmonious flower patterns in English gardens. (It was these theories, not entirely neglected in our own day, that were considered by the poet himself to have been his most enduring contribution to mankind.) Turner's later works – and Turner was an avowed disciple of Goethe's teaching – represent a similar search for Nature's laws, in his later paintings and his abstract studies of colour relationship. The spirit of Jean Jacques Rousseau, too, was hovering not far away.

Our definition of the English tradition, within which the Elmhirsts worked, as an instinctive feeling for what is 'natural' in a garden, can be still more clearly expressed by the addition of a further clause: "as it was taught and practised by its two greatest garden designers of the past hundred years". The Dartington garden owes an incalculable debt to the influence of William Robinson and Gertrude Jekyll, who deserve more than passing attention in our story.

Robinson's The English Flower Garden, *first published in 1883, went through twelve editions during the three decades that followed, and a well thumbed copy of this gardener's Bible, containing 1,000 pages of information and illustrated with hundreds of charming wood engravings, was to be found in many a living room that contained few other books. It is not surprising to learn that this man, who in a real sense gave the English garden to the English people, believed that the use of Latin names for English flowers – quite unknown until the last century – had "done infinite harm to gardening". "It is best," he wrote in his preface, "to speak of things growing about our doors in our own tongue". But, if he held to traditional speech, he did not reject all innovation in the art of gardening itself, and gave a warm welcome to the mowing machine, which was invented in the year of his own birth. And, in his insistence that gardening was an art, Adam's glory as well as Adam's curse, he cites a passage from Wordsworth – good vintage Wordsworth it is, too: "Laying out grounds, as it is called, may be considered as a liberal art, in some sort like poetry and painting; and its object, like that of all the liberal arts, is, or ought to be, to move the affections under the control of good sense".*

William Robinson (b.1838) was an Irishman of humble social origin who worked in exactly the period that ensured him a maximum influence upon his time – on people who made gardens (he had a very wide professional practice), on the theory of gardens (though self-educated, he was a prolific writer of gardening books) and, perhaps more than any of these, on his great contemporary in the garden world, Gertrude Jekyll. He was the apostle of the 'natural', loving wild flowers and pleading for their planting – their almost casual dispersal – even in carefully designed and formal areas. It was he who really brought about the fullest realization of the English garden dream as the nineteenth century dreamt it: he spoke to the increasing army of new suburban householders who had become enthusiastic gardeners. He wore his professionalism lightly, deprecating all paper plans and insisting that each element in a composition must be governed by the nature and contours of the land, together with its existing trees, plants and buildings – particularly these last, which were to be given their rightful place in the overall design. "A garden should grow out of its site", he used to say; and "The plan of a garden can be made only after its evolution, not before".

From his late thirties onwards he worked for many years in partnership with his near-contemporary Gertrude Jekyll, and together they effected the revolution in garden design. It has recently become apparent that he was the true originator of much that has been attributed to his distinguished protégée alone. Most of the scores of gardens for which they were jointly responsible belonged to large country houses with a staff of gardeners, but their writings were bought by the owners of smaller farm houses, even of cottages.

Robinson popularized all the old garden plants of the cottager, and he lived to see the style of the new movement spread all over the country: both gardening publications and personal interest increased steadily throughout the second half of the century. Forsythia, rhododendrons and azaleas are only three of the discoveries of that era.

Gertrude Jekyll came from an upper middle class Victorian family (which pronounced the first syllable of its name to rhyme with 'seek'), and received the education which was shared by most country gentlewomen of her time, including in her case some formal training in art and furniture design. She painted, she knew the artistic 'lions' of the day – Ruskin, Morris, Burne-Jones, – she wrote books, she moved among cultivated people. She was in her late forties when she first met Edwins Lutyens, some thirty years her junior, and began to advise him on the gardening aspects of the houses he was designing.

A long friendship now began; they realized that their talents were complementary, and their remarkable – and remarkably successful – professional partnership lasted for forty years. Between them they created over a hundred gardens. Their joint style was slightly more formal than Robinson's, possibly because it was based on more intellectual preconceptions. Robinson mostly called for the simply outlined border and more or less permanent plantings, while Miss Jekyll preferred a greater use of flowers, more colour and subtlety of form, and a fuller use of the wide range of trees, shrubs and plants that were being introduced into general gardening at that period. It has been said of her that she "translated painting into terms of gardening". In her colour schemes she was profoundly influenced by the Impressionists, in particular by Pissarro, Degas, Cézanne, Monet and Renoir. Any discussion of her pictorial sensibility must take into account her abnormal visual equipment: she was very short-sighted – as were Pissarro, Degas, Cézanne, Monet and Renoir. Indeed, myopia appears to have been almost obligatory among the great artists of the time, and many of them refused to wear spectacles as distortions of their 'real' vision.

While Gertrude Jekyll's great eighteenth century predecessors had planned for large landscape effects on the scale suitable for country estates, her own schemes were applicable to the tens of thousands of gardens that were then being made in the expansion of house-building for the ruling middle classes. Together with William Robinson she was responsible for the real social and aesthetic revolution that has been brought about in the homes of the twentieth century. She may also be fairly credited with the invention of the herbaceous border.

CHAPTER IV

FROM THE NEW WORLD

Beatrix Farrand came from a well-to-do New York family with strong literary connections: Henry James was a friend of her mother, and the novelist Edith Wharton, herself a keen gardener, was her father's sister. Beatrix Farrand had no formal education – there was little available to women in the United States of the 1870s – and she learnt her gardening, more through art than horticulture, during several years of European travel.

Stewart Lynch had only recently finished work on the Open Air Theatre when the Elmhirsts decided that they needed further outside advice. Gertrude Jekyll had died a few months previously in her ninetieth year, but they were in touch with Beatrix Farrand, a garden designer who was widely regarded as her American counterpart. To involve Mrs Farrand seemed the ideal solution, and in September 1932 they asked her to come to Dartington on her next visit to Europe, "in order to give us some general planting schemes".

Beatrix Farrand was then in her early sixties and, by general consent, America's most distinguished landscape architect (she preferred the term 'landscape gardener'). She studied painting in Paris in her early twenties, after living for a while in Florence and in Rome, and might perhaps have succumbed to the usual cosmopolitan lures offered to the comfortably-off Americans of her day: a Jamesian tourist's wandering existence in the great art centres of Europe, or what Edith Wharton called "the life of leisure and amiable hospitality" nearer home. Instead she returned to New York determined to become a professional gardener. Her first New York office was in her mother's home, and it was some time before the work could be described as a practice: rather it was a kind of cottage industry undertaken at the request of the many friends of her family. But from these small beginnings she went on to win a remarkable reputation, and by the early years of the present century her clientèle was spread right across the United States. Some of her finest work was done at Universities, the Princeton campus occupying her for thirty years on end. Her best-known garden, Dumbarton Oaks in Washington D.C., was created during the last twenty five years of her professional life.

She was no stranger to Britain. As a young woman she often accompanied her uncle, an ardent sportsman, on shooting trips to Scotland; she made a special study of Repton's great eighteenth century gardens, and on a visit to

England in the 1890s she went often to Kew Gardens and to Hampton Court, and admired the Tudor garden at Penshurst in Kent that Gertrude Jekyll had recently, to use her own words, "confirmed and renewed". She saw Vita Sackville West's first English garden at Knole; more important, she met the two people who most profoundly influenced all her later work, the ageing William Robinson and Gertrude Jekyll.

She was no stranger to Dorothy either, having long been a friend of her parents, and she had designed a magnificent garden in Long Island for Dorothy and her first husband Willard Straight. Work there began in 1914 and was still continuing for several years after the purchase of Dartington Hall. Dorothy paid occasional visits, but the garden did not long survive: in the 1950s the estate was sold and broken up into half-acre lots by a land developer.

Her work at Dartington was wholly in the English tradition as it had been cherished in the United States, and must be reckoned among the finest of her achievements. It differs from others in two respects: first, it was her only commission from outside her own country; secondly, a wide-ranging account of her career, published in America a few years ago by a writer who was familiar with Dartington (the book's sub-title, *Pioneer in Gilt-Edged Gardens*, may lend confidence – or may not) omits to mention it at all.

She paid her first visit to Dartington early in 1933, staying for nine days, and was delighted by everything she saw. She made the most of the experience, too, Dorothy subsequently saying of her that "She worked incessantly, scrutinising every corner and angle, setting up her stakes, taking meticulous notes, planning, planning every hour of the day and night ... In a short fortnight she had shown us the way to proceed".

Those few days meant everything to the Elmhirsts. She and they were agreed that the work should be taken in hand as soon as possible, and all the trees and shrubs, ordered by her before she left, were planted in the following autumn. But it was by no means an easy time, since the Dartington Trustees were about to assume financial responsibility for the 'Hall garden', hitherto Leonard's concern, and man-power was being reorganized. A new Land Agent, Jim Luard, was to exercise general control; David Calthorpe became head gardener; Stewart Lynch ceased to be Garden Superintendent and moved to the commercial side of the operation. There appeared to be more than a sufficiency of under-cooks to help stir the garden broth – and the head cook was living in a different continent. When it is considered that all her plans had to be carried out by means of correspondence, Beatrix Farrand's achievement becomes all the more remarkable: many hundreds of letters and occasional cables passed between the seven people involved over a period of five years.

It is true that the Elmhirsts crossed the Atlantic four times during this period, but these were mainly family visits. It is also true that their consultant came three times more to Dartington after her initial foray, but never for more than a fortnight on end. On the shortest visit of all – it lasted only three days – she was accompanied by her husband Max, a University Professor of History whom she had married in her early forties. Talk cannot have been only about gardens – time was needed also for the forging of the true friendship which they were beginning to know.

Shortly after her first visit she wrote to Dorothy: "If you like Dumbarton Oaks let us all three, Leonard, you and I, work to make Dartington its English fellow," and a few weeks later: "Let us allow Dartington to speak for itself, with its simple nobility of line and long human association." In her loyalty to William Robinson she never forgot that a natural garden does not result from leaving everything to nature, and her other great mentor, Gertrude Jekyll, was always sufficiently in her thoughts for her to insist that gardening was, in her own words, "something absolutely artificial". "It is the change from nature's scale", she once wrote, "that makes the composition artificial: a real garden is just as artificial as a painting."

Though she found herself forced to carry out her Dartington project almost entirely by remote control, she overcame the difficulties with an extraordinary sureness of touch. The sheer logistics of the enterprise were formidable enough: whether it was stone (of exactly the right kind), gravel (of exactly the proper colour), young trees and shrubs or even bulbs (several thousand at a time), every single order required her sanction, as the correspondence reveals. Her letters – many more to the garden staff than to Leonard and Dorothy – contain a flood of searching questions and a firm grasp of detail. ("I shall be interested to hear whether the bamboos have yet been moved away from the hillside near the theatre" ... "I shall be interested greatly to know what has been done about Priorities 1, 2 and 3" ... "You will doubtless remember that we discussed the question of an electric drill as an advisable investment for the wiring and training of shrubs on the walls of the Hall – has this been bought?")

Quite early in this period she asked that Stewart Lynch should be sent to the States so that he could discuss with her what most needed doing, and have the chance to visit some interesting gardens. In consequence, Lynch spent an action-packed fortnight as her guest. Shortly before the outbreak of war she

Above: the Courtyard as Leonard Elmhirst "discovered" it in 1925 and, right, the restored buildings seen in their modern setting. The pool of crocuses growing beneath the Turkey oak on the Great Lawn is one of Dartington's most famous sights in early spring.

said, in the course of a letter to the Elmhirsts: "I therefore suggest and really urge that Calthorpe be sent over to me next month". Leonard at once rang up the travel agency, and Calthorpe was sent.

The first problems that confronted Beatrix Farrand, during her five years' work at Dartington, concerned the condition and the proper visual treatment of the Courtyard. The area at the Great Hall end – a lawn that had quite recently been used as an adjunct to the private house – was still in fairly good condition; but the whole of the remaining space was sadly derelict, as the "snapshot taken in 1925" makes clear: Dorothy Elmhirst speaks of "releasing it from dividing walls and sheds, from pigs and poultry". Mrs Farrand grappled first with the discrepancies of ground levels and angles on both sides of the long axis of private house, Hall and kitchen, and dealt very skilfully with all the awkward slopes and intractable corners. Treatment of the garden side of these buildings was comparatively straightforward, and the South lawn was sloped off gradually as far as the 'arches', much as Tipping had earlier advised. In the Courtyard itself, where there was a fall of over 6ft between the upper and lower residential ranges, she dealt with the difficulty head-on by establishing a uniform level for the whole of the central area, and buttressing the entire wing on the lower side by building a retaining wall in the manner of a ha-ha. The proper elevation of the Great Hall, which had been distorted through the centuries by the gradual piling up of soil against the lowest courses of the fabric, was also now restored. Another bold decision was the elimination of the straight road running through the centre of the Courtyard, and the substitution of a circular drive close to the buildings. The creation of a central lawn at once unified the whole quadrangle. By laying down spacious areas of turf on both sides of the manor house, and effectively surrounding it with grass, she revealed it in its proper setting: in Dorothy's words, "the wide lawn in the centre of the Courtyard acts as a firm garden base from which the Great Hall arises". All the landscaping work was carried out under the supervision of Stewart Lynch, who had himself drafted plans for the clearance and re-design of the Courtyard, embodying a similar basic idea, which Beatrix Farrand was now developing. The surface of the roadway that encircled the central lawn was partly paved, by the use of local limestone throughout, and partly cobbled, following an ancient pattern which is believed to have been Japanese in origin.

The re-planning of the Courtyard had to take into account the trees that were already growing there, and a few others were now planted. There could be no question about preserving the 50ft-tall swamp cypress that had stood there since the middle of the last century. *Taxodium distichum* has been a guest in England since the mid-seventeenth century; in its native home in Florida it normally grows not much above sea level, in water-logged soil where the base of the bole is totally submerged during part of the year. The roots of Dartington's splendid specimen evidently find water somewhere here – Leonard Elmhirst supposed from a hidden spring. In the opposite corner of the Courtyard there had formerly stood a group of century-old Scots pines; only two of these now remained, and the Elmhirsts planted a number of others to keep them company. The group of four flowering cherries (*Prunus yedoensis*) standing at the archway end of the Courtyard was added in 1947. A fifth, near the entrance to the present Elmhirst Centre, became diseased and was uprooted in January 1987, to be replaced by a sapling that was planted in Dorothy's memory one hundred years to a day after she was born. The walls surrounding the Courtyard now show mainly silver and yellow colours. "The planting", Dorothy wrote, "was kept unobtrusive in order to enhance and not detract from the soft grey stone of the building. Climbers and wall shrubs have been used here. Nothing that would upset the beauty and the historical or architectural features was to be permitted – certainly no climbers that would damage the structure or upset the ancient lines. The planting had to support or embellish the buildings and walls, and not fight with the ancient grey plaster, stone or lichened patinas."

The Elmhirsts were anxious for the Forecourt – the whole approach to the entrance archway – to be developed as part of the Courtyard plan, but Beatrix Farrand seemed reluctant to tackle it. Eventually, in 1938, she did turn her attention – "under pressure", as Dorothy later recalled – to this area, where she was urged to find room for the parking of cars. She made the best use she could of uneven levels, but always regarded this hurriedly improvised plan as a temporary expedient only. The steps leading down to the side entrance of the Barn Theatre are of her design, but the outbreak of war in 1939 prevented the completion of her scheme for the whole of this area.

She then turned her attention to the main garden, beginning with the Great Lawn area and the plantings close to the kitchen and private house. She went herself to Hillier's nursery at Winchester to select the two cedars for the White Hart lawn, adding at the same time the libocedrus, the deodar and two large hollies in an effort to blot out the roof of the Dance School. She made careful lists of all the climbers chosen for the private house and the Courtyard, in

Above: the Camellia Walk that leads through Beatrix Farrand's Woodland.
Right: the terraces in early autumn framed by the great beech at the edge of the woodland.

particular the wistaria and the magnolias on the walls of the house. She began work in the centre of the garden by a certain amount of landscape lay-out, widening the Sunny Border and the path beside it, making steps at either end and further flights of steps from the Open Air Theatre to the upper drive and from the drive to the Woodland. She felt it important to have an alternative way down the hill from the High Cross entrance gate to the Hall, and constructed the path along Broadlears, joining at the top of the Heath Bank the little goat track, as she called it, that made a zig-zag down to the stream. At the same time she planted this track with many varieties of erica, and bay laurels on the inner side. She also designed the Children's Playhouse, now used as the Garden Superintendent's office, not far from the Garden Shop. She told Dorothy that she always enjoyed providing children with an environment which they could feel was peculiarly their own, and she envisaged both a playground and a special children's garden attached to the Playhouse. The plans were left in abeyance in 1939, and by 1945 had been forgotten.

The area where her creative touch was at its surest, and where her influence can still be felt most strongly, is beyond question the head of the valley, that before its clearance was always referred to as the Wilderness and is now known as the Woodland. It was for her work there that the Elmhirsts first felt particularly grateful to Mrs Farrand. "This development", Leonard wrote to her, "has been a constant nightmare to us, and we now feel that the garden has a backbone." Even during her first visit she had decided to replace the unsightly tangle of old and overgrown laurel bushes by interesting walks – three of them, roughly parallel with the old upper drive, a little higher up the valley – and to fill these with flowering shrubs. Anything growing here needed, in Dorothy's words, "protection from the ferocity of the western gales", but shrubs of sufficiently vigorous growth were found to accompany the surviving laurels in forming what was known to the irreverent as "Mrs Farrand's laurel and hardy garden". Although the removal of old wind-break growths certainly did expose this area to the powerful south-westerlies, it should be said that the garden as a whole, lying on the leeward side of the hill, is remarkably well protected from the prevailing winds. Beatrix Farrand's work at the upper end of it displays to full advantage the splendid trio of the Lucombe Oak, the ilex and the beech that towers above them both. She always insisted on using native material wherever possible, particularly as backbone planting – Scots pine, bays, broad leaved holly and beech. Each of the Woodland paths was characterized by special planting. The lower one was

flanked by magnolias and rhododendrons, the colour range being strictly limited to ivory and blue, with an occasional touch of pink, in order to bring out, rather than overshadow, the Davidia and the magnolias. The middle path was filled with camellias, and the top one (the Spring Walk) was enriched by masses of woodland flowers – anemones, scillas, violets and primroses.

Mrs Farrand also had plans to develop the area at the lower end of the garden, making full use of the stream and constructing a system of paths, but these were never carried out. She made, here and elsewhere, good use of ground cover plants – there is little bare earth at Dartington. But it is in the Woodland that the English tradition is perhaps most clearly seen: her American disciple had begun the planting immediately after a visit to the elderly Gertrude Jekyll, and her use of colour, together with the grouping of the camellias and magnolias in particular, undercarpeted with wild flowers, is an open tribute to what she had recently admired in the garden of Munstead Wood, Miss Jekyll's Lutyens house in Surrey.

An interesting light is shed on the nature of Beatrix Farrand by the survival of a single "statement of fees rendered, covering the period from January 1936 to June 1937". This was a fairly busy time: a large number of letters packed with instructions, questions and suggestions, was constantly crossing the Atlantic, and the Dartington project was clearly demanding a good deal of her professional attention. The account came to 159 dollars and 59 cents – say the equivalent of £40 – for a year and a half's work.

By 1940 it had become apparent that Mrs Farrand was unlikely to be able to continue with her Dartington project. There is a hint of finality in a letter that she wrote to England, to say that "working with you all has been one of the happiest experiences in what is now a very long professional career". But if the work was over, the exchange of letters continued, and there was never any question of her losing touch with developments in Devon. She was continually asking for news of trees – individual trees, even – and demanding copies of recent snapshots. One of her lists specified twenty four separate photographs, each to be taken from a carefully described position. These did not necessarily meet with her approval – "The pie-shaped piece of garden shown in your photograph worries me considerably: the paving looks to me unpleasantly small in its units". When she learnt, in 1941, that Dorothy had caused the rock garden (on the site of the present peat garden) to be dismantled, she wrote: "It always was a heavenly situation, but it was full of old-fashioned Victorian trash". If her dismissal of the rockery seems a little brusque, even contemptuous, we should recall that she was using a noun that is now obsolete on our side of the Atlantic, though evidently not on hers, a good sixteenth-century English word for garden growths of small worth. The only note of real protest to be found in all these years of correspondence – and it is a fairly mild one – occurs in the late 1950s, when she writes: "Please – no more *Juniperus Pfitzerianus*, they always look as though their locks needed combing out, and they just don't 'go' with the terrace." They very soon did, in the ordinary sense of the word, go.

Two areas in particular never ceased to cause her concern: the lay-out of the entrance Forecourt, and the loggia to the private house. One letter to Dorothy, written in old age, ends with: "Do try to solve the north approach to the gatehouse." It is not a gatehouse, but one sees what she meant: the area is still unfinished, and looks it. Up to a certain point the paving carries Mrs Farrand's clear 'signature' before it abruptly stops; and only the upper part of the Barn Theatre garden has been planned. The whole of this approach to the Courtyard has indeed the provisional air of 'work in progress'. It was always difficult to know what to do with visitors' cars, and we are a little shocked to learn, from a letter that Lynch wrote to Mrs Farrand during the war, that "parking spaces on either side of the Porch tower" were a possibility – nor did she positively forbid them, though she did declare that car parks inside the Courtyard at the entrance end were "most inadvisable". Ten years later the Forecourt could still be described as being "walled in on three sides, and now used as a parking place for cars and char-a-bancs"; and so it remained until Robert Hening enclosed it in the sixties with removable posts, and laid out ample space for cars a little further away.

Long after it had become clear that she would never see Dartington again, Beatrix Farrand would refer in her letters to small projects that had evidently been long forgotten there. During her 1935 visit, for instance, she had left instructions for the alteration of ground levels outside Leonard Elmhirst's study window, and the building of a low retaining wall. Early in the following year she went into precise details about what she wanted done, including the planting of "tiny rock plants or other almost microscopic objects – the work should be carried out carefully and with an understanding eye and hand". Later in the same year she wrote to Jim Luard: "I shall be interested to know if the little retaining wall alongside the Hall near Mr Elmhirst's study window has been built. This wall with its planting would veil the differences in level . . .". Four years passed, and she asked: "Has the little wall under the study window

finally been finished and planted?" Thirteen years later she was inquiring of Leonard Elmhirst: "How are the levels at the foot of the wall outside your study?", and four years later she was still hoping for an answer when she wrote to him: "The levels outside your working room were baffling, one wonders how they have been solved by you both and Mr Cane." This letter is dated 1957, when she was aged eighty four and still concerned about a few feet of low walling that she had last set eyes on twenty two years previously.

Beatrix Farrand's last letter, written not long before her death in February 1959, has a touching quality: past and present seem to be merged, as they often are with the old, but the uncertain use of tenses stops well short of mental confusion. "The loggia continues to be a difficult problem, it did not seem to fit, and yet the impression left on me was that it was a necessity and that the blame of its ill-fitting is *mine*." She died a few months before entering her eighty eighth year.

Dorothy Elmhirst wrote a memoir of her at the time, vividly recalling her first short visit to Dartington in the early 1930s: "No one who worked with Beatrix Farrand could fail to be impressed by her professional attitude to her job. Always the first to be out in the morning, she was the last to come in at night. Her energy seemed to be able to surmount any obstacle – even the worst onslaught of rain and cold. In her tweeds and mackintosh, we could see her tall, erect figure conversing, in all weathers, with architects, builders, gardeners, tactfully collaborating with them all and slowly winning them to her ideas. Not for nothing was she known among our friends as Queen Elizabeth. Her finely chiselled face and dignified bearing seemed indeed the personification of royalty. Her clear incisive mind was greatly enriched by her wide cultural background. Both in her professional capacity and as a friend and companion, she was in every way a remarkable woman."

CHAPTER V

GARDEN INTO LANDSCAPE

During the years of wartime the development of the garden had to be almost entirely suspended, and it became impossible to maintain previous standards. The numbers of outside staff sank to three; their work was restricted to the cultivation of vegetables, and to the barest minimum of upkeep elsewhere. What this meant to Dorothy can be guessed from a single sentence – a cry of dismay in a letter that she wrote to Beatrix Farrand in 1945: "There is long grass everywhere – even in the Courtyard." Yet these were days of enormous importance to her. She spent not less time in the garden, but more. She was often to be seen in the Children's Garden: "When the agonies of the war were all around us", she recalled later, "and when all my children were so many miles away, I used to work in their little garden in an effort to try and establish a link with them." Leonard wrote to Mrs Farrand in 1940: "D. spends hours with Mr Calthorpe, using her spade and trowel as a means of defeating Hitler, in the little time she has from caring for refugees." A little later she herself wrote: "Despite the war – or perhaps because of the war, I have begun to concentrate on the garden. I find I have a great desire to add to the permanent beauty of Dartington in these days when everything else seems so transitory, and I have never dreamed before of the satisfaction derived from work of this kind." This is a revealing statement in a revealing letter: it records a profound change in her attitude, not indeed to the natural world – her feeling for that had never been in question – but to this garden that it had meant so much to her to bring into being. Many years later she was to write something of the same kind in an even clearer – and more touching – way: at the close of a long evocative sentence written for one of her garden talks, she dwelt in turn on some of the places there that for a variety of reasons had been most precious to her, ending with the words "and somewhere the hint of a cottage garden, by the garden shop, because that is where I started in the war, it was my children's garden". 'Cottage garden' and 'that is where I started' make it clear enough: if

Beatrix Farrand was certainly aware of what was happening to her friend; in the 1950s she wrote to Leonard: "D has evidently caught the gardening germ, and she knows what intimate joy it gives to try to find out what the land and the site really want and need, and then to try to carry out its wishes as nearly as one can understand them." An affectionate note sent to Dorothy herself contains the assurance that "once your neck is in the yoke, the happy garden burden will never leave you, and will add joy to each day, since somehow the very humblest work in dealing with growing material seems to make one grow oneself."

ever there was a time in her life when she consciously chose – or was chosen by – the garden at Dartington, it was surely during those early wartime months. After that, she never looked back: increasingly, during the early post war years the garden 'held' her and was never to let her go.

While war continued, and the agony and suffering increased, she knew she must be patient – besides, there were so many other claims on her time. Yet the garden never ceased to call her. To Stewart Lynch, who was now a sick man and had retired in 1943, she wrote: "There is so much that I long to tell you these days about the garden. We have at last put in the final consignment of flowering cherries – four Tai Haku's near the White Hart ... I myself have been re-planting the children's garden, and working in odd corners as the weather permits. But of course anything to do with the garden is absolute heaven to me." A year later she wrote to a friend: "We do want you very badly to help us with the garden, and until you come we are holding up certain decisions ... I know it sounds very trivial and irrelevant these days to be thinking about a garden; but perhaps it is also a kind of salvation."

Soon after war ended, the garden staff was increased and general rehabilitation began. Six years' neglect called for the help of the Woodlands Department, together with its tractor and winch, to undertake tasks that were beyond the powers of the newly recruited staff. Johnnie Johnson had in 1943 succeeded David Calthorpe, and the title of Garden Superintendent was again in use. The Elmhirsts began their search for a successor to Beatrix Farrand, and their friend Constance Spry recommended the well-known English designer Percy Cane, who paid his first exploratory visit in the summer of 1945. He was then in his mid-sixties, and had established a considerable reputation as a Chelsea Show exhibitor and an author of 'garden books' based on travel in Europe, the United States and Japan. His books are readable enough – fluent and never lacking in self-confidence. When Cane first came to Dartington he had already made scores of garden designs for private land-owners and public bodies – a 'select list' of these mentions 82 in the British Isles, five in France and one each in the U.S.A., Austria, Greece and Ethiopia – this last being the garden of the Imperial Palace at Addis Ababa for the Emperor Haile Selassie, which was later to be described by an obituarist as "one of his most grandiose conceptions". The total number of his gardens runs into several hundreds.

Cane was born in a small Essex town, where his schooling was brief and promised little; he was in fact self-educated, and he took an unusually long time to grow up. When he started to earn his living at the age of twenty two

it was as a subordinate in a metal window factory. In his late twenties, having steeped himself in Ruskinian theories, this serious minded man, nourished by the highest ideals, attended an Art School for a while, but he did not take kindly to the coarseness of speech and behaviour that he encountered there, and at the age of thirty he began to write articles for an occasional journal called *My Garden Illustrated*, of which he became editor and owner three years later. This looked like the beginning of a possible career, but the date was 1914 and the war years were to find him working in the Food Production Department of the Board of Agriculture, writing leaflets on the spraying of potatoes. So when in 1919 he at last went into practice as a landscape and garden architect (his own chosen term), he was nearly forty. It is difficult to avoid the words "slow developer" in speaking of someone who was to write his first novel at the age of ninety.

Success was long in coming, but still it came. He rented his own studio in London, but he never took a partner. Physically small, teetotal and a bachelor, he found in his deep dedication to Art all the spiritual nourishment that he needed. He loved music, particularly opera, and he once told his biographer that it always helped him to solve a design problem if he listened to great masterpieces: "say something from The Ring for a severe design, or, if I wanted sheer beauty, some Mozart. Then the problem would solve itself without any effort on my part". His favourite relaxation was foreign travel, almost always to Greece and Italy to gain inspiration from studying the works of both classical antiquity and the Renaissance.

Harry Tipping had come twice to Dartington, and Beatrix Farrand four times; Percy Cane was to pay more than fifty visits, and during the whole twenty three years of his consultancy there were only two when he never came at all. In his busiest periods he would usually make four visits each year, more often than not staying overnight in the private house. He began work at Dartington a little shakily, and tried to do too many things too quickly: Dorothy confided to her diary: "Mr Cane is suggesting so much change that I feel bewildered – he even wants Davidia to go!" This was perhaps the most precious to her of all the trees in the garden. Before very long, however, she was won over by his obvious integrity and total dedication to his calling, and she was often to write in later years: "How I bless Mr Cane!"

He recalled in one of his books that on his first visit to Dartington he had "realized that its wonderful possibilities had not been fully appreciated ... There was no clear way to make a tour of the grounds ... The visual relation

The Tai Haku cherries, among the garden's special treasures, were planted at the suggestion of her friend, Will Arnold-Forster. All existing specimens of this white cherry descend from a single bush found in 1923 in a Sussex garden, to which it had travelled at the turn of the century in a consignment of fruit from Japan. It was Arnold-Forster, too, who in the late 1940s counselled the generous planting of Malus hupehensis. To Dorothy these flowering crabs were a source of particular delight, bringing to the Meadow what she once described as "a cloudlike effect of pure whiteness in May".

Percy Cane

of vistas to the scenery beyond the confines of the gardens left very much to be desired". It would be difficult to quarrel with any of these propositions. His first aim was – as indeed Beatrix Farrand's had been – to strengthen the links between various areas of the garden. It was still a collection of parts, not yet a whole. The Elmhirsts were looking to him to restore to order, and to improve upon, the work of Mrs Farrand that had suffered so severely during the war years. This was exactly the kind of work for which he believed himself best fitted: "Dartington Hall", he declared not long afterwards, "is not for the conventional type of garden – it demands landscape on the grand scale". No one would describe Cane as a miniaturist.

His overall plan, which permanently changed the nature of the garden, included eight distinct yet interrelated projects, most of which were carried out between 1946 and 1957. To make the Glade, he began by cutting through the thick wild overgrown upper areas between High Cross Hill and the Heath Bank. Here he created a broad sweep of grassland flanked by shrubs and a few of the best old trees, to create the first of the vistas by which he set such great store. What is now the Glade had formerly been a tangle of undergrowth, but when Cane had finished clearing it, a splendid view was revealed of the medieval buildings and the lower part of the garden, and beyond these into the Devon hills. There were some who had loved this almost secret area where one could lose oneself; but Cane had come to allow the garden to breathe – he flung the windows wide to let in the air, and parted the curtains to let in the light. You could not have both mystery and clarity, and the Elmhirsts were firmly on the side of their new consultant.

In order to link the Glade with the rockery at the foot of the Heath Bank far below, he built, during 1947 and 1948, a long steep stairway of Yorkshire stone that led down from Moore's newly sited Reclining Figure to the lower end of the Tiltyard, flanked by bays, magnolias and groups of erica. He was at pains not to impose it on the slope, and to avoid the appearance of rigidity by the mere mathematics of its construction: the 71 steps are proportionally rather wide and shallow, the nine separate flights are of different lengths (4,7,8,9 or 11 steps) and even the width of the landings varies from 5ft 7in. to 3ft 6in. Cane rightly described the stairway itself as an essential part of one of the largest vistas created by him at Dartington: walk slowly down from the top to the bottom of it, and the magnificent view changes slightly with every step you take. There are still those who remember the old pathway down – Beatrix Farrand's "little goat track" – and regret its loss; but, given the right conditions of light and colour at many times of the year, the boldness of Cane's design can silence criticism and work a magic of its own. Some see in the stairway one of the garden's most powerful features; others concede the power but regret the price paid for it. Opinion is – and is likely to remain – divided.

Though Cane was not really a 'trees man', he was careful in the Dell to introduce a variety of ornamental trees, juniper , Japanese maples and azaleas among them, in order to maintain a proper balance with the existing mature specimens of native trees, always with the same aim: to open up new vistas, to guide – even to surprise – the eye "towards some special feature, a temple, a view of the hall, a glimpse of a piece of sculpture". He would not have claimed special gifts as a plantsman; sympathetic critics of his work found his management of flowers sound enough but in no way original. He rightly saw himself not as a horticulturist or a garden designer, but as a landscape architect.

The view from the Bastion. The paved area is also known as the "whispering circle".

The area known as High Meadow had recently been used as a cutting garden, and looked in general rather like an out-of-town allotment. Cane cleared it completely, to create a quiet enclosure with trees, and an opening towards the Hall, here disclosing yet another vista. He called High Meadow "a garden for summer and autumn". Further down the valley he planted the higher part of the Orchard Field with Japanese cherries, acers, oxydendron and scarlet oaks, to give autumn colour.

He laid down York stone paving in front of the private house and along the terrace at the upper end of the Open Air Theatre, with a stone seat at its southern end; he also made a semi-circular stone path below the Theatre, to connect the Heath Bank with the rockery. One of his happiest notions was the building of a circular stone look-out platform near the top of the Heath Bank. It has been variously described as a rotunda (though it is not a room), a bastion (though it has no military purpose) and a belvedere (an attractive word, but it surmounts no building). Whatever it is called, it gives a wonderful view over miles of Devon countryside to the south east. Percy Cane was a man for all vistas. Dorothy recalled it memorably when she wrote: "From the Bastion, just above the stairway, the ground falls away to the parkland and over the hills toward the sea. The land in the distance seems to take the form of soft green waves, silently rolling in".

In an attempt to complete the plans that Beatrix Farrand left unfinished, Cane next gave some attention to the Forecourt entrance to the Hall. The area had defeated her; it now defeated him. He dealt boldly enough with the upper end of the Forecourt by planting what he described as "some columnar

growing *Juniper chinensis* standing clear from the upper wall at regular intervals on each side". He hoped that in time they would form buttresses of green, thirty or forty feet high, giving an Italianate character to this approach to the Courtyard; but they were never given the time. By the early 1960s they were removed, and replaced by twelve Leyland cypresses, now at their full height, standing very close to the wall and to one another. If these are really an improvement on their predecessors, Cane's first thoughts must have been seriously at fault. The general appearance of the area was largely saved by the planting, at about the same time, of the pair of Chinese Maidenhair conifers that now flank the steps leading down to the Barn lawn. All the existing specimens of *Ginko biloba*, long revered by the Buddhists of southern China, are the sole survivors of a species that flourished some two hundred million years ago, and remains of identical trees are often found in coal seams laid down at that time. They were introduced into Europe in the mid-eighteenth century.

His work a little lower down the hill shows Cane at his most successful – his most reticent. The only section of the entrance drive that had not been obliterated during the late twenties was now, as he rightly declared, "lacking in dignity and quite inadequate", and in its place he designed the present gateless drive that "follows an easy curve between mown lawns on either side", making full use of the park-like setting surrounding the eastern elevation of the Hall and presided over by the great Turkey oak. Beatrix Farrand was pleased to be sent a photograph of the new drive, and wrote to the Elmhirsts: "Evidently in Mr Cane you have a wise and understanding adviser." What Percy Cane thought of his predecessor's work we shall never know: nowhere, in his printed lecture on the garden given before the Royal Horticutural Society, or in the many pages of his books that refer to Dartington, does he mention her name at all.

Responsibility for this part of the garden was in fact shared between them, since the plantings on the Great Lawn are mostly attributable to Beatrix Farrand. Some preliminary work had been done during the early clearance years , and Leonard Elmhirst describes the felling in 1927 of an enormous oak tree growing much too close to the great Turkey oak that now dominates the lawn. The garden staff believed that it was diseased, and he reluctantly consented to its removal. It proved to be "as sound as a bell, and had a perimeter at its base of nearly 30ft". Beatrix Farrand believed strongly in the planting of sizeable trees and was pleased to find that a large silver Atlantic

The pool beside the Azalea Dell, the garden's only sheet of almost still water, photographed in winter and, right, in autumn. It is fed continuously from springs and contains the curious, ever flowering water hawthorn. (For some the use of water in the garden has always been too modest in scale. See page 56.)

Not the least engaging of Percy Cane's contributions was one that he was never allowed to make: the creation of substantial areas of water garden. In 1958 he thought he had found a good site for a pool in the Valley Field, and put forward a scheme for bulldozing out a pond, making a dam in the ground below the Garden Superintendent's Office. The plan shows a series of linked pools at the very bottom of the garden (roughly in the form of a club hammer with a rather bulky head). Dorothy Elmhirst was sceptical, and nothing happened. A year later Cane offered to come down and stake out the pool; a year later still an amended plan was being costed.

After a further seven years interval he tried again, this time addressing the Elmhirsts publicly by writing in his Creative Art of Garden Design: "A stream runs through the centre of the meadow, and it has not yet been decided whether the water should be dammed at the lowest level to make a small lake." Still nothing happened.

In 1969, at the age of eighty-nine, Cane had a last fling. With splendid pertinacity he suggested a site for a rather smaller area of water surrounded by an 8 inch stone kerb to be located opposite his long stairway. It was to be adorned by "various figures on pedestals" – or an alternative might be "a fairly strong jet of water". Leonard approved the site, but gave himself room for manoeuvre by adding, "I do

cedar had been brought to the Lawn only a few months before her first visit to Dartington. The actual journey had not been a long one – from a garden only a mile or so away – but the work had been done without the aid of a transplanting machine, and the tree was 25ft high, rooted in a ball of soil weighing over a ton. She lost no time in telling Stewart Lynch of the tree-shifting techniques, involving the use of canvas jackets, that were then being practised in the United States. Her own plantings included two other cedars, a Himalayan Deodar and a cedar of Lebanon, of the kind that was introduced into England in the mid-seventeenth century. The great Turkey oak, which Dorothy Elmhirst considered to be one of the finest trees in the garden, is much older than its companions: *Quercus Cerris* was first planted in England by an Exeter nurseryman in the mid-eighteenth century, and the one at Dartington could well be an early immigrant some two hundred years old.

Cane's enthusiasm for 'opening-up' wherever possible is well illustrated by his treatment of the Valley Field. Until he began work, the 'gardened' part of the estate had ended below the Heath Bank, and a rough fence – wire supported by stakes – had separated mown grass from open field, well above the point where the little stream that rises in the Azalea Dell, only to disappear again within a few yards, becomes visible once more before taking its final dive into the rocks. The whole of the Valley Field was taken into the garden in the late 1950s, and planted along its top ridge with trees and flowering shrubs for colour. Cane had always thought that the ground below his stone stairway was without definite form, and sought to make a better transition between the garden and the parkland into which it imperceptibly merges. He finally solved his problem in the best possible way, by doing nothing at all. There is indeed a line on the map where garden ends and farmland begins – it even has a modest hedge to mark it – but the ditch makes no attempt at all to declare a boundary, and the garden never actually ends.

Most of Cane's work for Dartington was concluded by the early 1960s, several years after his official retirement at the age of seventy, but his professional visits to the garden became hardly less frequent. In the early years of his consultancy these had followed a fairly uniform pattern: he would arrive during the early evening, and discuss plans with the Elmhirsts over the dinner table. On the next morning he and Johnnie Johnson (until the latter's death in 1963, after which it would be Terry Underhill) would make a careful tour of inspection. Full reports – models of their kind – were always made of meetings held to discuss the garden, at which Cane was invariably present, even in his

not think Dorothy would have stood for any of your charming figures". Dorothy had died two years previously.

It was the final skirmish. Over the years water gardens of one kind or another have been suggested for every possible area of the garden: at the head of the valley where the little stream first makes its appearance, at the very bottom where the garden ends, rather higher up the Valley Field, and higher up still just below the Tiltyard. There is nowhere else for water to be, except the Tiltyard itself, and that is surely unthinkable. Yet someone did think of it seriously: the illustration shows quite clearly what Percy Cane intended, and may be left to speak for itself!

old age. During the post mortem on a short-lived waterfall in the Valley Field it is clear that there was a general determination not to be unreasonable: "Mr Cane said he felt that the whole feature, although extremely well done, was entirely wrong in that position ... Mr Elmhirst said that the waterfall could never have come there naturally, although he liked it very much... Mrs Elmhirst agreed with Mr Cane on most points ..." Some of the reports amount to little more than 'Minutes of the Meeting held', but many seem to be almost verbatim and run to between 2,000 and 3,000 words. A few excerpts may serve to paint the scene, and they are evidence that Percy Cane was not content with a non-speaking role. When he is not calling for a new water feature (of his own design) he is often to be found emphasizing the need for more "points of interest, say a fountain or a piece of sculpture", and the phrase "No decision taken" is sure to follow. [1961] "Mr Cane advised the planting of a forest tree – perhaps a lime or an Austrian pine off centre in the middle of the Forecourt, in order to hide the roof behind it. Mr Elmhirst remarked that Austrian pines only grow 2 ft a year." [1961] "Mr Cane said he knew he would meet with opposition here." [1961] "Tour of the garden with guests. Mr Elmhirst observed that we were now entering that part of the garden which he called 'a memorial to Percy Cane'. Mr Cane thanked him, but wondered perhaps if the epitaph was a little premature. The party then moved out of the Glade." Cane was then nearly eighty. [1961] "Mr Cane held to his opinion." [1964] "Mr Cane voiced his dislike of the deep yellow colour to be seen by the stream, as it did not blend with the other colours in the Dell. Mr Underhill said it blended when looked upon from the opposite direction. Mr Cane disagreed. No decision taken." A delightful period touch is provided by the same year: "Mr Cane pointed out that the Church Tower, as seen from the Bowling Green, appeared in two shades, light and dark, and he suggested that it would be better presented all in one shade. Mr Underhill to remind Mr Elmhirst to speak to the Rector about it." (This tower stands not in the garden but in neighbouring Church property.) [1966] "Mr Cane said that something more than pure nature was needed here; he would do a sketch." [1966] "Mr Cane said that all garden curves should be convex, not concave." It is pleasant to learn that his last visit to Dartington was a happy one. He came in the Spring of 1968 when he was eighty four, to discuss the planting of trees that would screen the new dance-drama buildings from the Hall: "Mr Cane drew a plan which was gladly accepted by all those present". Of all the gardens on which he had worked, Percy Cane considered Dartington Hall's to be the

most interesting, though he may have been prouder of his own design for the British Pavilion at the New York World's Fair in 1939. His name is now forgotten, and a wide gulf separates much of what he stood for from most of what commands assent today; yet he deserved well of his generation – and of Dartington. His judgment may sometimes be questioned, but never his sincerity, or his total dedication to the work in hand. The Elmhirsts and he established over the years a working agreement that was perhaps unexpected but proved to be as successful as it was enduring. Neither his loyalty to them, nor their generosity to him, seems ever to have faltered. They used his real gifts, and curbed his worst excesses, with understanding and with tact, and hardly ever failed to draw out the best that was in him. Dorothy in particular always listened to Cane's suggestions, and was usually prepared – sometimes even anxious – to 'give him his head'. The lavish deployment of *Juniperus Pfitzereanus* to which Beatrix Farrand had taken such strong exception ("they look as though their locks need combing") was none of her doing: they were Percy Cane's special favourite, and he told Dorothy that in his opinion "the

more ragged they look, the better". He once persuaded her to plant a row of flower beds over the entire length of one of the terraces – pink, red and blue hyacinths in serried blocks. This was admittedly a short lived experiment, and by the following season they had all disappeared. Leonard provided the following reference for Percy Cane when he was – it is a little surprising to learn – at the age of eighty three seeking employment with Devon County Council: "He has worked for us for about 18 years . . . In working out his plans bit by bit, we came to realize the remarkable sense of design that was characteristic of his approach, and I think he has never made a mistake from the design point of view". This was, it is true, a reference written to a prospective employer, and we do well to remember Samuel Johnson's dictum that "in lapidary inscriptions a man is not upon oath"; all the same, there is no reason to doubt that it represented Leonard Elmhirst's settled opinion. Dorothy paid her tribute to him as a gardener in the following terms: "In his planting schemes Mr Cane adhered to his own basic principles of design, massing shrubs of the same sort together and arranging colour combinations

Facing page: two views into the Valley Field, the larger to show the richness of early autumn colour. On this page: Percy Cane's steps seen in relationship to the equally firm geometry of the terraces and as a foundation for magnolia blossom in spring.

that helped to emphasize and not detract from the essential form of the planting. He has tried to give full value to the architectural features of the garden, believing in the importance of space, and of relating lawns and trees and shrubs to each other in a formal composition". This was never the story of cultivated land-owners allowing a gifted and occasionally wayward garden designer to put his pet theories into practice: it was at its best a true partnership. The Elmhirsts certainly received good help from Percy Cane, but they also encouraged him to achieve the best that he knew. No one is in a better position to understand the 'inside' story of this professional-personal relationship – during a shared undertaking, let us remember, that lasted for more than twenty years – than Victor Bonham-Carter, who wrote in his *Report to the Trustees* that "it must be emphasized that the inspiration behind the rehabilitation and redevelopment of the Hall Gardens came in largest measure from Dorothy Elmhirst herself, who – with Johnson's practical help – improved the detail of most of Cane's plans, especially the blending of the colours, but above all brought vision and perception into every aspect of the garden's progress". Percy Cane's Indian Summer was a long and not altogether happy one. His consultancy was never formally terminated, and in his mid-eighties he was a guest at Dartington only six months before Dorothy died; but after the rejection of the Pool with Figures he paid no further visits, although letters continued to be exchanged from time to time. After one unusually long gap in this correspondence, Leonard wrote with some garden news and his letter was returned marked 'Gone Away'. It turned out that Cane had, six months previously, had a severe stroke and was being cared for in a Home. His mind was wandering, his affairs were in a muddle, and after payment of his outstanding debts the capital sum left would not keep him for more than twenty weeks. Leonard made sure that the old man was given the creature comforts that he needed. Cane in fact lived on for many further months, and finally died at the age of ninety four, surviving his benefactor by almost two years.

CHAPTER VI

A GARDEN IN FLOWER

Two major features of the garden remain to be described – the Tiltyard, and the statues and other ornaments accumulated over a period of more than thirty years. The re-conversion of the Open Air Theatre into its original form as a tiltyard was carried out during 1954–55 by a garden staff that totalled twenty. (For many years thereafter their numbers remained at this level, or slightly below it; today the whole area is looked after by three full-time gardeners, with some trainee help.) Lynch's theatre had been the cause of considerable heart searching, beginning quite soon after it was built: the purposes for which it was originally planned had simply not been fulfilled. The unfavourable Devon climate was chiefly to blame, so that in the first twenty years of the theatre's existence only two evening productions had been given, an all-night Indian dance performance presented by Uday Shankar and his company by the light of a full moon in the Spring of 1933, and Shakespeare's *Julius Caesar* given by the Elizabethan Theatre Company on a midsummer evening in 1953.

Other, less urgent, reasons had contributed to the decision to re-plan the whole area: the cutting of the grass had always been a problem, and the existing levels were awkward and difficult to manoevre, being too high to serve as steps and so ill adapted to walking up or down. Dorothy Elmhirst had summed it up in curiously strong words: "The theatre is a kind of dead space in the centre of the garden". She had long felt that, from the point of view of its design, the hard horizontal line of the yew hedge behind the stage was disturbing, cutting right across a downward slope into the valley beyond.

Once the decision to abandon the Open Air Theatre had been taken, the plan for the development of the whole area quickly gathered momentum. Dorothy Elmhirst wrote that it would be "turned back to its historic fourteenth century form as a tiltyard, flattening out the whole space to the level of the present stage with a steep flight of steps at the top. An opening will be made in the yew hedge to clear the view down into the valley and to enable

Left: workmen restoring the Tiltyard in 1954. On this page: views in high summer and early spring of the dramatic empty space created as a result of their work, "the central feature to which everything else must be related".

Of all the things that were planned at Dartington during the early years of the 'experiment', one received no mention in this chronicle for the good reason that it was never carried out. But since it closely concerned the area under discussion, and since it might conceivably have given the centre of the garden a strong and permanent flavour of teutonic architectural "Modernismus', it deserves to be recorded here. In the early 1930s Walter Gropius, one of the most influential designers of his era, was seeking to establish a studio in London "to secure a unified character for the products of Dartington", as he put it. Nothing came of the project, and how far Leonard Elmhirst went along with the idea it is difficult to say: the whole story is by Dartington standards ill documented, and a little mysterious as well, particularly where it involved the garden. When Gropius left the celebrated Bauhaus, and Germany, under the Nazi regime in 1934 he was invited to visit Dartington, and the place had cast its spell on him: he was in fact in two minds, whether to make England his permanent home or to begin a new life in the United States – as a few years later he did. He was the Elmhirsts' guest on nine occasions within a space of fewer months during 1935, and was actually asked to draw up a plan for a stone-seated open air theatre. This looks like a piece of 'impulse buying' on Leonard Elmhirst's part: Lynch's laboriously constructed garden stage had been completed only three years previously, and in the event Leonard went no further than giving the plan his general approval ("We like the idea for your theatre expressed in the sketches") and suggesting that its position should be shifted slightly, "so as to leave the existing theatre more or less as it is". Gropius's plan provided an auditorium for 604 people, with "room for 40 additional seats around the forestage if necessary", thus amounting to over three times the seating capacity of the present Barn theatre. The 'aerial perspective view' reproduced here is by another hand: Gropius himself was a clumsy draughtsman, and actually disliked drawing.

Dancing in the Tiltyard at Dartington's first Foundation Day celebration in 1943. Published in PICTURE POST *at the height of the war, the image was meant to give "our men overseas a contrasting picture of English country life".*

people to walk through to the lower paths that connect with the rock garden and the heath bank. Communication will thus be opened between different parts of the garden, where hitherto it has been blocked. It is also hoped to place more seats in what will be the sunken tiltyard, and because of its sheltered position these seats should prove welcome at all times of the year."

Beyond acknowledging that the acoustics were superb, no one had a good word to say for the Open Air Theatre. Leonard declared that it "never really worked. The weather, the midges, the dew, the coldness of most summer evenings in South Devon, all combined to destroy such other charms as there might have been, scenic, romantic or acoustic. For the rest of the year the area was unsuitable for anything".

The work of dismantling went ahead, in accordance with Percy Cane's instructions. The thick yew hedge that grew right across the lower end of the theatre, now a good 10 ft tall, was no longer fulfilling its original function as a backdrop to the stage. A central gap was cut in it, and the height was everywhere reduced. A new drainage system was installed, and the whole area was re-sown with Chewing's Fescue grass, to give a sufficiently tough surface to withstand folk-dancing or games.

The centre of the garden became a tiltyard once again. Leonard had always been sure that John Holand had once jousted there, and Dorothy reported with obvious pleasure that "we have preserved it in its noble simplicity and in its historical dimensions, 70 x 40 paces, settled around 1380 by Thomas, Duke of Gloucester as the most appropriate size for jousting. We have resisted the insertion into it of bedding, of borders or of lagoons in the face of much pressure". (Is she possibly enjoying this passing smack at the still untiring local champions of the water garden? She cannot have known when she wrote this, that several more episodes in the Dartington Lagoon Show, already described in these pages, were still to come.)

The first two mock tournaments to be held in the restored tiltyard were staged on two successive Foundation Days in 1957 and 1958. They were also the last two. No seats were ever placed there, since the central greensward, although it is sometimes invaded on festive occasions, has never become a place to sit in or, as Dorothy envisaged, to walk through. This is, inescapably, the central feature of the entire garden, to which everything else must be related: it is making an historical as well as an aesthetic statement, and clearly Dorothy was hoping that it would one day be fully used; but as things have turned out, her phrase "a kind of dead space" is as apt as it was when she first

The sculptor is here looking, it has been said, at the human form metaphorically: the figure is as much Nature as Woman, with its supporting arm and shoulder "shaped like a blunt unyielding promontory". Moore himself chose the site for the Figure, and his choice caused no little surprise at the time. He wanted it to be looked at against the skyline, in contrast to the common assumption of the time that a piece of sculpture should be discreetly enclosed, whether by building or vegetation. Many people hoped that it would be moved, but the only practical suggestion came from Percy Cane, who suggested to the Elmhirsts that it might look very well if it were placed at the lower end of his own 'Sunken Formal Garden'. The suggestion was not accepted.

wrote it thirty years ago. No doubt she was right in asking Percy Cane to design a stairway approach to it, but the only thing to do, in fact, when one has reached the bottom of these spacious steps, is to turn round and walk to the top again. Few of those who are familiar with the garden would wish it otherwise.

The garden is particularly fortunate in its statues and other ornaments, both for what they are and where they are. All deserve more detailed treatment than the mere recording of the dates of their acquisition, which are spread – in the case of the statues – over a period of fifteen years: Willi Soukop's Donkey (1935) and Swans (1950) and Henry Moore's Reclining Figure (1946). Willi Soukop is of Austrian and Czech parentage. He first came to Dartington in 1934 by chance acquaintanceship, knowing no English, and worked there for a while as a freelance sculptor and part-time teacher of sculpture. The first work of his to be installed in the garden was the Donkey, cast in bronze and mounted on a blue limestone base quarried in Buckfastleigh. Dorothy Elmhirst had offered him, for use as a studio, the little thatched summer house designed by Rex Gardner in 1929, and he first modelled the Donkey in plaster at the suggestion of Stewart Lynch, for exhibition in the Dartington stand at the Chelsea Flower Show of 1935. In 1950 Dorothy asked him to design some sculpture to incorporate the old granite cider press that was already installed in its present position as a fountain, with a jet in the centre of the basin and linked to the mains water supply. Having often admired a couple of swans sailing on the Dart, he needed no suggestions for his subject. During a single day at the Bodmin Moor granite quarry he chose a 2 ft cube, drilled a hole right through it, and with the centre thus fixed developed his design around it. This was his first experience of carving in granite, and the work took several months to complete. In their early days the swans looked rather too new for the ancient weathered base, but now the moss that covers them needs constant scraping away. In his writings, Percy Cane always refers to the sculpture as "the Swan": he took it to represent a single bird with two intertwining necks." Henry Moore's Reclining Figure in Horton stone was specially designed to stand in the Dartington Hall garden, as a memorial to his friend Christopher Martin, the first Arts Administrator. For two successive years the sculptor had found it valuable to be working simultaneously on two quite dissimilar carvings, the other being also a reclining figure, but in elm wood: the wood, he found, demanded fluid lines and, by the very nature of the material, a sense of movement and growth, while – in his own words – "one of the essential facts

The statue of Flora among daffodils in spring.

about a block of stone is its weight and immovability". He once described the wooden figure as "dramatic", in contrast to the "rather gentle, calm and peaceful" Martin memorial. The Dartington sculpture may be regarded as a partial retreat – or was it possibly an advance? – from the near-naturalism of the great Madonna and Child that he had carved two years previously for the Church of St Matthew's, Northampton. In 1959 Dorothy suggested to Percy Cane that some sort of architectural 'feature' should be designed to stand at the head of the Glade; she spoke of it as the Glade Temple, or – in less classical mood – sometimes as a small summer house. Cane submitted his ideas for a pavilion, and his drawing survives in the Dartington Records Office, with a note attached: "Mr Cane's plan for a summer house. Turned down, and the job given to Robert Hening. – L.K.E." One aberration such as this should not be held against any man, and is best forgotten – Cane made no claim, after all, to be an architect. A not unkindly colleague later described it as "a sketch for a Cotswold bus shelter".

Bob Hening's design was inspired by the so-called Temple of Fortuna Virilis in Rome (the fickle goddess is described as 'manly' through a verbal confusion with Portumnus, god of harbours). The building is of Portland stone with some flooring of Buttermere slate. The pantile roof was crafted by an old Somerset tile maker, and the specially designed lettering on the slate plaque reads: "In 1960 this building was given by Leonard and Dorothy Elmhirst to commemorate the happy fellowship of many years with the Trustees of Dartington Hall." Underneath the site chosen, which had been cleared on Percy Cane's instructions during the making of the Glade, there was a formidable tangle of large tree roots, which it was found impossible to remove completely. Hening was taking no chances, and the stability of his pavilion should be ensured for a very long time by the solid block of reinforced concrete, at least 4 ft in depth, on which it stands.

When work on the temple had begun, and the scaffolding was already in position, Percy Cane paid a visit to the scene, and the Gardens Minutes faithfully record his reaction: "Mr Cane", we learn, "did not appear entirely to approve the design", and he made a practical suggestion that was no doubt intended to be helpful: "he thought the site of the building should be moved one foot to the left, and the base slewed round a little ..." (Eight years later, on a visit to Dartington at the age of eighty six, he told Leonard Elmhirst that the Garden needed two more temples and that he was ready to offer designs, but "would not act without instructions".)

The statue of the minor Roman garden deity Flora, a late 17th century figure cast in lead, was given to Leonard and Dorothy by the Dartington community on Foundation Day 1967. Funds were collected from all over the Estate, and the maximum contribution was fixed at 6d. The statue's position, at the end of a pathway near the top of the garden, could not be bettered. Percy Cane persuaded Leonard to let him place ball finials on the pre-existing stone piers that flank the entrance to the pathway. The suppliers were taken aback by the size that he asked for, and protested that a diameter of 1 ft 5 in. was the maximum that could be mechanically contrived. Cane stuck to his 1 ft 11 in. design, and in the end the finials had to be carved in York stone by specialists masons at an enormous cost, each of them requiring a solid block weighing well over half a ton.

The sub-title of this book does not, of course, imply that the narration ends with the completion of the work; as Dorothy herself wrote: "No garden under active cultivation is likely to achieve a final form, and each year Dartington undergoes minor changes. Whether by overcrowding, or damage wrought by gales, or by the natural process of decay, plants must often be rooted out and new varieties introduced. Experiments are continually being made; in fact, so continual is the process of change that any description of the garden which aims to give an exact and permanent arrangement of plants would be deceptive." It is clearly impossible to say that at any given point this garden was finished; but it should be possible to use some such phrase as 'a garden in being', and the year 1961, though it may seem to be rather arbitrarily chosen, has some justification in that Dorothy then felt able to write her short guide to *The Gardens at Dartington Hall*. From that date onwards, it can be said that the garden had quietly assumed its acknowledged place among the finest to be made in this country during the twentieth century. Gardens do not compete. If they were amenable to any kind of league table, such a table would be remarkably difficult to draw, since those belonging to one category alone – gardens that are open to the public on one or more days in the year – number well over a thousand. Each of them is unique in its character, but they can be said to group themselves into certain basic kinds. Thus no one would describe Dartington as a flower garden, no one would rank it high as an exhibition of botanical rarities.

Every visitor will have noticed that there are very few single specimens at Dartington: whatever is planted has been planted in masses and groups. Both Dorothy and Leonard were ill at ease with any small patch of garden that was unrelated to its surrounding, and always preferred to plant on a large scale, following the lines of the land itself and making the garden less a series of delightful parts than what it is now generally regarded as being, an unusually satisfying whole. And they shared the same high standards: there is no poor material to be found anywhere – nothing that Beatrix Farrand could possibly have called trash. Percy Cane once declared that Dorothy Elmhirst had the most critical eye for form that he had ever come across.

When they came to Dartington in 1925, the Elmhirsts had not even any gardening friends; twenty five years later they could talk with experts as equals. Certainly, as we have seen, they sought advice from many other people, both friends and professionals, but though these might often suggest the plantings, the actual material planted was always their own choice. Dorothy made scrapbooks containing photographs of gardens and articles describing them. She read widely, and built up in the course of the years an impressive library of garden books. She and Leonard rarely ordered plants direct from the catalogues, but preferred themselved to visit the great nurseries and to learn all they could from practising horticulturalists. Over the years they paid many visits to the great gardens of England, sometimes linking several of them in an extended tour of inspection. In the words of a friend, "they knew their English gardens pretty well". Dorothy was generous in her appreciation of some, not uncritical in her comments on others: of one of the most widely respected she wrote in her diary: "Disappointing because so messy: a few things looked nice". After they had been to Sissinghurst, with which Dartington has a number of close affinities, Dorothy wrote a delighted letter of thanks and sent a Mandevilla as an assurance that the visit had been "a complete and perfect thing". They were disappointed to be away when Vita Sackville West returned their call, but she still asked if she might come "as an ordinary tourist, with a card of permission from you?".

Dorothy wrote of Dartington in 1961: "This is a garden where form has dominated design and where compositions have been attempted, using the contours of the land to intensify the natural effects of height and depth and distance. Trees and shrubs are used to give structure to the compositions, and lawns to emphasize space. We had to lay out paths and grass to hold the whole rhythmically together; our final task was the connecting of the garden with the distant vistas of hill, valley and agricultural field. In the early years the whole place was so shut in. We had to discover a thread of relationship that could tie the immediate intimacy to the distant aspect in a natural and harmonious

manner. Flowers we have with us somewhere all the year round, but in winter look at our magnificent evergreens, bays, hollies, yews, box, rhodos., Scots pine and ilex, mixed with leafless decidous giants. What delicious composition they create, what varieties of texture".

CHAPTER VII

THE GARDEN NOTEBOOKS

The making of the garden occupied Dorothy Elmhirst for more than thirty years, and she was to spend another ten years in developing and improving it. She made great changes along the way, and her garden in its turn made great changes in her, but it should not be forgotten that gardening was only one of many interests in the course of a long life. Her early advocacy of social reform had been tireless and radical, and her later literary and artistic pursuits were serious and informed. The mere burden of her unusual upbringing in New York's 'high society' at the turn of the present century must have been a heavy weight to carry. She became motherless at the age of six, and lost her father when she was seventeen, thereafter living continually in the public eye. She swam in a goldfish bowl where the fishes' scales were of real gold; she inherited a very large fortune from her distinguished politician father William Whitney, and became in her own right one of the richest women in the world. She travelled for many years in many countries; she "met everybody", but social life was always less important to her than the life of the mind and of the spirit, and her personal quest for a truth that could claim her whole loyalty, embodied in all she tried to achieve at Dartington, was lifelong and unflagging. How often it was in the garden that she most clearly discerned this truth must remain her secret, but it was increasingly here that she hoped to find it. When she left the house, trowel in hand, everything else could be forgotten, including appearances: she might wear her oldest clothes in the garden, and it was a place of refuge from importunate visitors. To work in the Rockery, or the Sunny Border, was to become perhaps the most complete escape that this genuinely shy woman ever knew – an escape into, not from, reality. As a friend once said of her, "Dorothy discovered happiness on her hands and knees".

During the whole of her long life she never wrote anything with the intention that it should be read by the general public. In 1961 the Dartington

trustees issued her admirable short Guide, The Gardens at Dartington Hall, which – with successive alterations and additions by other hands, made forms and remains in print. She also used often to contribute articles to the series of duplicated sheets known at Dartington as News of the Day, but these were read by an even narrower circle. In a strict sense, therefore, her 'collected works' are non-existent; but her own words, by degrees more intimate and revealing, can still be listened to in the pages that follow.

The first transcript is the only one that survives of several talks about her garden that she gave from time to time. It was not something she much enjoyed doing, but she would occasionally consent to address a small group informally at a friend's request. This talk was given to a party of teachers gathered at Dartington in April 1960.

Nature is our greatest source of beauty and in any approach to any garden we must start with a careful assessment of the gifts with which nature has already endowed us.

In the Hall garden the slopes and unusual contours are natural and our first task was to work out the best treatment for them. When I look at 'Country Life' I say to myself sometimes, "We ought to have made of it a romantic kind of a garden". But we also wanted, and we decided, to combine the classic with the romantic, the formal with the informal.

Take a look at the terraces, the old grandstand for watching the jousting below. When we came all kinds of alterations had been made. The garden had been played about with quite a little – a pit for baiting bulls and bears with dogs had been dug at the lower end of the jousting ground, and acres of laurel planted for shelter for pheasants. Leonard was quite sure it had been a jousting yard. All along we had a feeling that this area should be treated formally. First we replaced the pit with a stage and an open air theatre, but it never worked satisfactorily. Then we decided to return it to its original fourteenth century simplicity. The whole form seemed to become clearer.

The area below the arches in front of the house we call the bowling green. It was already formal. We kept this whole part simple with lawn and evergreen, yew and ilex and myrtle, all of which helped to marry the old grey walls into the garden without fuss or clutter. This formality we extended, leading up to

Dorothy Elmhirst had a number of favourite areas of the garden, but beyond question the Sunny Border was the most precious of them all. She valued it in particular for its unassertiveness, and said of it: "I have always had to keep the colours here quiet and restrained – grey foliage plants, cream, pale yellow day lilies, blues and purples when I can find them. It is the quieter colours that seem to suit our garden best, I think." She was always conscious of this personal preference for quiet colours, and tended to be half-apologetic about it: "Have we kept the whole too subdued? How difficult it is to put in a strong orange or a hot yellow! What a problem the reds are, alongside yellowy greens!"

the terraces and to those great Spanish chestnuts, four or five hundred years old.

From there on we decided the garden could be wilder and more romantic. The great trees themselves are so wonderful, ilex, beech, Spanish chestnut, Scots Pine, and Turkey Oak. But we had still to clear away a lot of clutter, often hiding the boles of these wonderful trees. We were ruthless and called in tractors and bulldozers to our aid, because in this garden it is form that counts, pre-eminently. Form is terribly important, every tree must count.

Then came the question of the landscape around us. Should we shut ourselves off from it or extend and open out into it? Some gardens, that are not in lovely country, feel they must concentrate on the within and shut themselves inside their surrounds. But here I feel that, to the East and the South, the sea, which is so near, is rolling in upon us, and is suggested by the rolling green and wooded hills around us. So we set out to open up new vistas into the distant country.

How could we best relate the old buildings and courtyard to the garden and bring them into an organic harmony? There is something so warm and soft and subtle about these grey buildings. So we kept the immediate garden low in colour and in tone, feeling that the brighter colours, reds and oranges, were not at all right, too garish. They didn't fit in.

Mr Percy Cane came to help us over the contours of the garden and showed us the advantage of intensifying the great heights and depths. He said you must take full advantage of the dramatic contrasts you have and that have been smothered or lost to view.

Perhaps, and for some people, it is wrong to talk in terms of a garden at all because we have so few flowers. But a sense of composition counts so much more than flowers here, and contours, lawns, noble trees and vistas all play a vital part. To keep this sense of composition right and alive I go out every day and want to move some shrub or plant. But I don't yet go quite as far as a Chinese friend of ours who begged us to hang a heavy weight on the big branch of an old Scots Pine which, he said, "to be right must be a few inches lower" – in a garden you never come to an end of the little extra touches that are needed.

Selection! How important this is! To choose one thing and not another, to concentrate certain kinds of planting in one corner and not in another. Cherries, magnolias, rhodos and camellias all in their appropriate places, the Sunny Border to reward us in July.

The second transcript – a selection of extracts from Dorothy Elmhirst's garden diary – is of a different order, and on a different scale. She kept this personal record, the equivalent of an artist's note-book, during the whole of the last twenty-six years of her life, entering her comments at regular intervals in a series of attractively bound booklets, each covering roughly one year. The complete diary is very long – something approaching 150,000 words – and much of it consists of a working gardener's notes, memoranda, lists of plants to be ordered, jottings of every description, material that could appeal only to a horticultural specialist. But there are also pages of delightful, totally unselfconscious writing that reveal to us a good deal about the garden and even more about the diarist herself. The choice of entries, that together span some ten thousand days, has been simplified by the existence of a skilful digest undertaken by Robin Johnson, who worked for many years in the Dartington Records Office. The entries themselves have been left unedited, except for the occasional insertion of names in square brackets, to make the writer's meaning clear to fellow gardeners. Dorothy Elmhirst is not preparing a text for the press – she is not even considering the effect of her words upon a reader. What follows is in fact not communication at all, rather a private act of adoring contemplation.

MARCH 1943 The most perfect of days – warm as midsummer – mown grass, birds and my large garden hat. Everything soaked in sunshine that burns.
... Continuation of Midsummer Madness! *Clematis armandii* Apple Blossom is exquisite delicate blush pink – but the one on the pillar by steps to Open Air Theatre is not too happy ... We badly need some more magnolias standing out in the grass against dark backgrounds – not enough blossom to be seen ... *Stellatas* are wrongly placed – should be against yews or something very dark.

JULY – The real excitement of the past week has been the opening of *Magnolia grandiflora* on the study corner and by the morning room. Jerry brought one branch actually into his study. What a flower – what utter purity, and never have I seen such smooth texture and such rhythmic curves of the petals, and added to the visual beauty – such an unearthly scent – the essence of lemon. How noble this flower is.

SEPTEMBER – A lovely planting day. Calthorpe and I put in crocus under three old pines in Courtyard ... Then we planted three groups of *Colchicum* above grassy bank of rock garden ... We also put in 4 sets of cyclamen in rock garden ... Then 2 doz. mixed *Erythronium* ... This p.m. we planted 200 bluebells.
... Planted out 48 white foxgloves, 24 Lutz hybrids in Wilderness. Took up all violets in Dell – forked in peat and replanted them, adding 12 Princess of Wales. Moved *Daphne mezereum* to new place among hellebores.

1944

MARCH – I walked today to Staverton Vicarage and back. Three things took my eye, the maroon tone of the alders against the deep blue of the river by Staverton Bridge; the shining faces of periwinkle peeking out from the hedgerows (I am afraid they are by nature wild!), and white *Arabis* climbing over the rocky ledge of a cottage garden in full bloom, with white and purple crocuses above – a lovely combination.
... I've lost my heart to the white *Erythronium* like a large open star.
... We've been having tea outside every day for the past week, and guests have been lying out on the grass in full sun as if it were midsummer. I've never known such a March, absolutely dry.

APRIL – The small group of fritillaries in the rock garden seems more fascinating than ever. We must have more.
... Had a thrilling morning examining leaf buds bursting out of their sheaths – the tiny leaves all wrinkled and crinkled (like a baby) from being folded up so tight.
... The smell of wistaria fills my room at night – so strong it is that I feel it must be in a vase beside me .
... Have been slaughtering snails in their ledges.

MAY.– Coming back after nearly a fortnight I feel that I have suddenly stepped into full summer. It was Spring still when we left – now everything has burst into the richest exuberance. The loveliest thing of all is our Davidia, so much better than any Davidias we've seen at Kew and Westonbirt . . . Made great mistake to put London Pride at corner of rock garden steps. That whole corner is bad.

JULY – The *regale* lilies are my greatest joy, and Cornus and roses and honeysuckle – oh, how I love the smell of honeysuckle . . . I mustn't forget the St. John's Wort that is a glorious blaze of colour all over the ground and along the steps to the Open Air Theatre. It is really a lovely flower.

SEPTEMBER – Did a little planting today – 1 doz. *Cyclamen ibericum* under beech by second seat on Rhodo Walk, 2 doz. *Fritillaria verticillata* under two great planes on old drive, 100 Snowdrops –

nivalis single under *Lonicera fragrantissima* by steps to Open Air Theatre, and 100 *nivalis Imperati* and *Atkinsii* in Courtyard under *Viburnum burkwoodii* and the rest between our kitchen door and the second back door into Hall.

NOVEMBER – A glowing warm day. Worked on Sunny Border putting back plants William had taken up in order to improve soil . . . A kindly negro soldier helped by wheeling away all the rubbish. . . . After three days in the house I've had a walk! There's a breathless stillness everywhere, and the silence seems to intensify the colour of the beeches . . . One of the best sights of all – the oaks across the valley towards Totnes. The real straightforward English oaks I imagine. There never was such a beautiful autumn at Dartington, or perhaps I was blind before!

1945

JANUARY – We've had nearly four weeks now of icy weather. It is so cold that one feels the whole world is held in a vice – paralysed, immobile. First we suffered from extremes of wetness – floods unprecedented – and now from unbroken and unrelenting cold.

. . . At last and suddenly the weather has changed – the wind is from the West, the sun is shining – there are shadows again on the lawn, the birds are singing, the sky is blue, the earth is soft and yielding. What an ecstasy it brings to our frozen hearts.

. . . This is proving an historic winter as far as weather is concerned. On the night of the 25th we had 18 degrees of frost up here at the Hall and 22 degrees at Central Office. And yesterday another violent snowstorm coming from the South. Today the snow lies deeper than I ever remember it here. The bamboos are lying flat on the ground and all the evergreen shrubs are bent over into the contorted constricted shapes of old age.

JULY – The smoke bush is a dream – *Rhus cotinus Purpureus* – in full flower, like spun sugar dipped in claret. I love it madly. The group of blue hydrangeas in the Loop is a great success and *Cornus kousa* is my greatest joy of all. *Cornus capitata* is having a sabbatical!

A few explanatory notes concerning people and places may be of use –
Bill: *son of Dorothy and Leonard.*
Chalet: *holiday home of the Elmhirsts and their children, a chalet built into the cliff at Portwrinkle, Whitsand Bay, Cornwall.*
Ghond: *Pet name for the Monterey Pine.*
Jerry or J: *family name for Leonard Elmhirst. We need not be surprised by the frequent references to Dorothy's absence from Dartington: she and Leonard were often out of England for a month or more at a time, and there can hardly have been a single year spent entirely in playing their role of the Squire and his Lady. The main diary is full of opening phrases such as* "Returning from ten days in Antibes", "Just back from three weeks in U.S.A.", "Jerry is in Tanzania", "Jerry still in India" *or* "Coming back from Venice".

SEPTEMBER – We've started with a vengeance making the glade from Upper Ranges down to Heath Bank. The tractor pulls the trees with little effort. So far a larch has come down – 2 oaks – 1 fir. We are also pulling out the bamboos in the Dell.

OCTOBER – Tremendous clearance is going on by means of the tractor. Great chunks of stuff pulled out of the Woodland, and the Dell, and, of course, the new Glade. We are going to see our great trees at last. I hadn't realized how terribly cluttered they had been.
... These are the days! The perfect autumn days – absolutely still, slight frost in the morning – hot sun at midday and a deep blue sky. Mr Johnson and I planted the Loggia yesterday – putting in tulips . . .

NOVEMBER – After a few days in London it seems as if a great change had taken place here – so many leaves have fallen. Only the beeches glow with the sun on them – burnt orange. They are so wonderful – the beeches. And now two beeches have been cut down – it's agonizing – one up the drive that was rotting away and the other in front of Johnson's house – also dangerous. But they've left such gaps – irreplaceable.

1946

JANUARY – Yesterday I studied buds – Lady Alice Fitzwilliam is about the

loveliest of the Rhodos – somewhat like an azalea bud – crimson folds edged with white. Then *Sorbus sargentiana* is fascinating – sticky crimson buds with long antennae. Magnolias have sheaths of mouse-grey fur around their buds and Davidia has nuts that hang by crimson cords.

... Strange light on everything today – with white earth and dark sky. The planes looked tawny and the beeches and oaks very dark grey – all the values were changed as if under the spell of an eclipse.

FEBRUARY – ... But there's no doubt that certain things do not look right while beech leaves are on the ground. I want to remove all snowdrops from Rhodo Walk for that reason – they should spring out of grass, not out of beech leaves, I'm sure!

MAY – After all, this is the high watermark of Spring beauty, with the beeches just emerging into that indescribably fresh green – and the oaks so ochrey, and the red *[Acer] palmatum* the perfect foil for all the different greens ... But there's one bad mistake in the Rhododendrons – Mt. Everest is too coldly white and too large in flower to be placed near augustinii.

SEPTEMBER – Back from U.S. to find a hurricane has laid low many of our precious trees – 1 chestnut near end of Rhodo Walk, the beech up the drive, several elms, branches torn off oaks and beeches everywhere. The planes seem to have stood best and fortunately Ghond and the Ilex by the Hall and the greatest beech of all on steps to Woodland survived ... But now that the ruins have been cleared away I'm thankful so many valuable things have escaped.

OCTOBER – Great excitement – the *Lapageria rosea* outside White Hart maids' dining room has flowered. Lacquer red wax-like long bell with white stamen, most effective.

1947

JANUARY – Returned from London at 2 a.m. in the midst of an American blizzard. Today in walking about the snow came above my Wellingtons. And yet the air is warm – that devastating east wind has ceased to blow. Papers say this is the coldest spell for 60 years or so. We've been feeding the birds – would we could do the same for our tender trees and shrubs.

FEBRUARY – Four days of deep snow – food brought up by sledge – no cars, no buses – only Joe Maitland's van to do the essentials. Floods in the house – 3 a.m.

MARCH – William and I have been transplanting all the orange crocus up to top Broadlears Walk. We've tried hard to make a natural effect. This morning we settled the exact spot for Henry Moore's figure.

JUNE – Mountain ash in bloom – good effect but horrible smell.

SEPTEMBER – We are having a kind of Sahara drought. The grass is quite burnt and yellow and the ground like rock. I've never known five unbroken weeks of sunshine before in England.

1948

MARCH – After a week of cold days we are having sunshine again – and though east wind blows the sun warms the earth and makes the birds to sing and the heart

of man to rejoice. Our first lawn mowing of the season – the grass looks so tidy and even and aristocratic.
... *Rhodo fargesii* is out – awful puce pink – let's remove it.

APRIL – A dream of beauty – the 8 Tai Hakus on White Hart lawn. They really are something quite apart – even more wonderful than yedoensis.
... I realized yesterday that it is shadows which add so much to the beauty of everything. Now that the beech leaves are out the trees are beginning to cast shadows – and it gives immediately a kind of variety and subtlety and mystery to the whole scene. I think this must be the perfect moment – just when the beeches burst into leaf.

DECEMBER – Heart lifting day after rain. Raindrops hanging along small branches like tiny silver bells ... I love *Cotoneaster simonsii*. It retains its tiny red and yellow leaves, and with orange berries it gives effect of stained glass.

... J. and I saw, in the light of the moon, the cherry *subhirtella Autumnalis* in its fragile delicate bloom. These moonlight nights have been quite unearthly – absolute stillness. Mild softness in the air – and the white roof of the Barn Theatre glistening like snow. Late at night we walk about – nothing seems to have weight or substance – all dissolved into thin air.

1950

MARCH – Such a glorious moment. The cherries are like something entirely outside of previous experience. Yedoensis with long arms of thick white snow – I have never imagined that blossom could grow so tightly packed along a branch – and the form of the branches too is unlike anything I have ever seen. And this year Tai Haku is out at the same time. It is unbelievably lovely – with the touch of bronze leaf at the tip. Seen over the yew hedge they look like snow peaks emerging out of dark forests in Switzerland ...

1951

JANUARY – At last the weeks of ice cold days have ended and the rain has come and the soft west wind. And with the change in weather has come a change in colour – from a hard frozen thinly coloured scene the richness has returned, with the deepening of the browns and reds and the warmer tones of all the different greens. Especially have I noticed the trunks of *Acer griseum* – of Rhodo Penjerrick – the cinnamon bark of forsythia and the lovely warm tones of even the *Mariesii* [hydrangea].
Prunus sub. Autumnalis is out, but not luxuriating yet.

Suggestions:
1. We must change the line of grass vista from road to Swans – too straight.
2. Must change lines of top bed in High Meadow. It comes out too far.
3. Lines of upper bed in Dell too fat and round.

MAY – Continuous wind and rain – never have we had such a Spring! Everything so late!

JUNE – What a strange year! The ordinary shrubs are so poor in bloom – like laburnum and Philadelphus. Whereas roses are fine!

1952

JANUARY – A lovely sunny day – warm when sheltered from the north wind – a deep blue sky and a lovely clear atmosphere. Hiram, Julian Huxley, Jerry and I strolled through the garden for an hour before lunch ... The blue hydrangeas retain colour but it has become a soft sea-green blue. Somewhat unnatural, Julian says, but rather fascinating.

MARCH – Jerry home again! Walked in garden last night, and this morning in soft rain. Bill and I examined pulsatillas. He remarked on way in which they hold raindrops that glisten and sparkle in their grey fur.

APRIL – Suddenly – as yedoensis and *Prunus Incisa* and *Mag. denudata* were about to burst into richest bloom they have ever had – an icy storm blew up – a cutting wind from east and snow and desolation. The poor cherries have been blasted, and many of the magnolia goblets browned.

The Monterey pine (called Ghond by Dorothy Elmhirst) after the ravages of the 1952 storm and as it looked when in its prime.

DECEMBER – Tremendous rain here, and ice and snow in other parts of England. Marvellous clear cold sunny day. The English oaks still have their copper foliage and are wonderful with the sun shining through. From top of steps the contrast is so beautiful of the dark evergreens and the grey of the White Hart wall.

. . . A disaster has befallen Ghond – two days ago Mr Johnson noticed a crack in the trunk – then, last night, on Christmas Eve, about 11 p.m. – Jerry and I, from the study, heard the fatal sound of its fall. Despite rain, Jerry went out with a lantern and found half the tree gone – fallen back against the bank. The front part is still strong and firm but the other half – on the terrace side – has split off and fallen – no harm done to any other trees. Like the chestnuts, these trees seem to know how to fall with the least damage to others, but oh – it is crushing to lose so much of our noble Ghond.

1954

JANUARY – No one seems able to understand the change in our climate! Up until last night we've had mild, soft, gentle weather – with the quiet expectancy of early Spring – and no feeling of winter at all – in fact it has been so warm that one can sit outside in the sun

without an overcoat. We saw a man today eating his lunch on the road – at the top of High Cross Hill – as if he were enjoying a summer picnic. Will all the flowers and shrubs be lured away by this false springtime in the air – or are they wiser than we?

MAY – Two really warm days – tea out of doors – cotton dress on – Joyful!
... This is the peak of the year, the ecstatic month when each day brings a deeper realization of beauty. The beeches – a maze of quivering green – as we sit on the Loggia and look through these screens of beech – one behind the other as far as the eye can see – Eleagnus like foam – pale green. Wonderful scents everywhere – Eleagnus, wistaria ...

OCTOBER – Mr Cane's visit today – to plan change in Open Air Theatre. We cut opening in hedge to see angles. Mr Cane wants to take first two side screens away, and will send drawing for lines of back hedge. Cut wider opening in low hedge at top – to allow for wide flight of steps. Mr Cane wants to eliminate two tulip trees for views above and *Cercidiphyllum* and Liquidambar which he thinks will block view into valley.

1955

MAY – After 3 months of illness I am back in the garden sitting on the Times seat with Jerry. Everything is so late this year that even today the beeches are only just in leaf and, as always, they seem to be the great experience of Spring. Work goes on in the new tiltyard – levelling still.

AUGUST – What a marvellous July – warm – day after day – sunny – still – absolute heaven for me – lying out on the Loggia for my rest. I can't remember any month like this before. August has been a miracle too – a succession of warm sunny days – sometimes as hot as 80 but usually in the 70s. Farmer goes on working on the new steps into the tiltyard – a slow job.

1956

APRIL – Dreadful things are happening to the garden. Frost has browned off the Magnolias and for the first time in my memory the big soulangiana looks bruised and flowerless. Also *Rustica rubra* above – and those on Rhodo Walk too. Then the cherries are a disaster – due to birds. For the first time they have taken the Tai Hakus and even *Shirotae* and, of course, the *[Prunus serrulata] Spontanea* – no cherries – and the Magnolias ruined and Rhodos too. The lovely owl-like white one – Arizelum – near Davidia – is now brown, and Yellow Hammer and others finished – oh!

MAY – A slight change – indications of warmer weather – the garden has never been so full of birdsong. Jerry and I wandered happily through the Valley Field planting and the little wood over the bank – all so nicely cleared. The Valley Field is full of new plants, and the view of the Heath Bank is more like a flight to heaven than ever – with the Magnolias and tall heaths so glorious together.

... Rain at last – the refreshment shines everywhere. Suddenly all the bluebells have appeared, both wild and tame – and the Spring Walk is a lovely sight still, with white and blues as ground cover. I mean white bluebells and blue ones both. Rhodo Walk at its best – the colour is really lovely – cream and pink and the wonderful blue of *augustinii*. The shape of it is so heavenly too – the big one by the beech ...

1957

MAY – Three *loderii* on loop in Woodland are just about the most glorious Rhodos I've ever seen – huge flowers and such fragrance! Thanks to a happy accident we planted them extremely well – with the strong pink at the back. Patience is pure white – quite overwhelming – and King George is pale pink – and then the more intense pink behind makes a marvellous group.

Left: the Tiltyard before and during the levelling of the Open Air Theatre in 1955.

Above: Jousting in the Tiltyard on Foundation Day in 1957. Medieval life was the theme of the annual estate celebration that year.

JUNE – Foundation Day. Unbelievable day – warm – no wind – soft – heavenly. Pageant – tilting in tiltyard – tremendous success. Border looks nice, roses good.

DECEMBER – Disasters! Frightful gale last night from South but twisting and whirling like a cyclone – 80 miles an hour in sudden ferocious gusts. Our losses are terrible:

1. Scots Pine in Courtyard.
2. Deodar on terraces.
3. Beech – upper drive above Sunny Border.
4. Davidia – split in half.

Fortunately the Scots fell along the path toward Barn Theatre and not against East Wing. Deodar fell downward into tiltyard, beech across upper drive against bank – damaging, of course, many shrubs and the fine young beech.

... It's dreadful to see the Davidia – as if a human being had lost both arms – the wonderful branch gone that came over the drive and the branches on the upper side. I can hardly bear to see it without crying. Somehow the other losses are less mutilating – cleaner and more complete. The Scots in the Courtyard has been sawn off at ground level and the Deodar too is being cleared entirely. Devastation

remains on the bank above the big beech on the drive – young beech gone and some Rhodos. Thank heaven the 2 old *augustinii* are safe and the Magnolias, and Lady Rosebery miraculously unharmed.

1958

MARCH – Glory, glory, halleluja! *[Magnolia] campbellii* is in flower! Large pink blooms at the top – against a blue sky – a sight long awaited and now ecstatically enjoyed. There seem to be about 30 blooms in all and all gathered together at the very top – a wonderful sight from the distance and marvellous from below.

... What a delusion of Spring those mild days brought us last week. Since then we have had 20 deg. of frost and bitter cold north wind ... But *campbellii* is now brown and so is *[Rhod.] cilpinense* and *Magnolia soulangiana* has brown buds, and *denudata* – oh! oh! Shall we be deprived of our early Magnolias as well as of the early cherries and forsythias? Frost is as deadly as bullfinches and sparrows.

APRIL – My heart sinks when I look at all our cherries – poor Tai Haku with only the occasional flower here and there. It seems that all the cherries have been stripped – what are we to do to protect them?

1959

MARCH – Despite east wind and cold nights *campbellii* is more glorious than ever – Bill and Jerry and I sat on bench under it for nearly an hour this morning. When the wind blows the white of the inner petals is almost like flecks of foam on those glorious waves of deep pink against a blue sky. There must be about 100 blooms – almost all like a bouquet at the top being offered to heaven. More blue anemones coming out.

... The yedoensis are today in bloom in the Courtyard – so incredible – palest pink – a delicate fullness of bloom, so extraordinary – I can't believe it. And I see from my bed the yedoensis by the Heath Bank. *Campbellii* is still a glory – paler now in colour but still there. From the Henry Moore figure *campbellii* shows up best of all – because from that point it has a dark background. What a wonderful revelation for us this year – *campbellii* and yedoensis.

MAY – This has been the day of days – perhaps it only comes once a year. It was so hot I could not sit in the sun on the Loggia at tea time. What a moment for the garden! Azalea Dell – quite perfect – brilliant, glorious and yet all in keeping with everything else. Eleagnus throws its scent far and wide. An intoxication in the air. Hundreds of bees humming within those myriad branches ...

Suggestion: Far end Woodland – too many bluebells – move some over to opposite side. We must be careful not to encourage too many of the red primulas either – on the lower side.

NOVEMBER – Sunday with J. to see the effect of the opening into our ancestral English park. I think I love it almost more than any other feature of English gardens. The fence has been removed in the Valley Field and now there is the great sweep down and then up to the first little hilltop where the monkey puzzle stands and then on to the farther hillsides – all in soft gentle waves to the far horizon. The oaks, of course, give the ancient character to this new parkland of ours. They are so right – so immemorially right.

1960

JANUARY – Wet – wetness everywhere – 2 months of rain – but some lovely things to see.

... Snow – snow suddenly and deeply – no cars can dare the hill save with chains. Two casualties in the garden, Eleagnus has lost a branch bending over the road and *[Pinus] insignis* by old 3rd tennis court has a branch down.

DECEMBER – Tree surgeons doing dangerous work both on old chestnuts and on themselves.

1961

JANUARY – More wet – the poor earth is sodden – but work still goes on. The tree man goes on filling holes with tar – one Scots in Courtyard now being treated – the beech on Rhodo Walk. The Walnut on high terrace being cut down.

MARCH – A night of heavy frost – 11 deg. – has done fearful damage – poor *[Mag.] denudatas* are brown and the big *soulangiana*, with which was one huge multitude of buds, has been battered and bruised and terribly hurt – I can hardly bear to look at it.
This morning we planted all the lace-cap hydrangeas on the old Forsythia Walk. *Aspera Macrophylla* and Blue Wave *Macrophylla* 8 ft. – tallest – then the *serratas* along edge and at corners ...
Also today Alford and a boy have begun to take up turf from our front lawn – for Mr Amery's excavations.
Turf restored on news that excavations are postponed.

DECEMBER – Walking through Woodland I was struck by the openings

Mr Johnson has made – *Pittosporum* gone and other protecting greenery. It leaves precarious open spaces for wind but will, of course, allow more sunshine to penetrate Spring Walk.

1962

MAY – Bluebells thick mass – lovely. Returning from London after 4 days absence – the whole scene has changed – everything has come at once. I think this is the most utterly moving and beautiful moment I have ever known here. Oaks, beeches, even the chestnuts and planes are coming now – and the great beech at the top of the steps – from the terrace looking down I wondered how everything could be so overwhelming and yet real. Davidia

and Eleagnus wonderful – and the Dell – oh – what richness. I am amazed at the success of the colour – I can't find anything to change!

NOVEMBER – I had forgotten how beautiful the ground becomes below the trees as the leaves fall. Reluctantly I watch leaves swept away from terraces and upper drive.

1963

MARCH – Returned 2 days ago from New York. Landscape brown – all way down in train – lawn here is greener than any grass I've seen anywhere. Two days of rain – but milder than I expected. Impossible to be certain yet of the garden casualties – probably the Acacia in the corner of White Hart and the Olive – but though *Cornus capitata* looks ominous and *Mag. delavayi* and others – they may recover greenness.

1964

MAY – The perfect Sunday morning. Great moment with beeches in their shimmering young freshness. At top of drive at High Cross I rise to heaven with the beeches.
... Eleagnus – what a scent! I forget from one year to the next how overpoweringly pervasive and sweet it is.

JULY – A marvellous month of warm sunny days – we shall soon be complaining of drought.

Suggestions:
Dell – needs something – not even lilies now – dreary sight.
Circle – too much white – why not floribundas here?
Loggia too bare – only scattered purple petunias.

Courtyard – too bare – yellow dahlias good but they need the grey plants I had hoped for.

NOVEMBER – Leaves all swept away. I can't help regretting the glowing carpet below the acers and cherries and the glorious flood of colour from the planes down the terraces.

1965

MARCH – Hundreds of people in the garden on this first perfect day of Spring. Warm sun and no wind. The stillness brings such peace. And now people wander down the stream – in fact everywhere you look the place is thick inlaid with humans – and dogs and prams and cameras and all the happy paraphernalia of a Sunday out – out into the Spring.
Courtyard – yedoensis in corner by old gym is full out – as usual it brings a kind of breathless adoration. The others should be out in a few days – I love them in the fullness of their bud as they are now. It was the use of a gun that has frightened off the bullfinches.

JUNE – Several shocks:

1. Occidental azaleas by Davidia. So wrong in one big group . . .
2. Another shock – Sunny Border. When everything was taken out to enrich soil –plants were put back without any plan – chaotic now and not at all my original plan. Day lilies have gone and Delphs – and other treasures – and too much *Anchusa* no – no – Anchusa fine.

OCTOBER – The best days of the year – east wind – but windless! Walked alone by Valley Field and hopefully but disastrously back – by a tangle of nettles. Found right path into upper level – higher up . . .

. . . The moment when flame-coloured leaves of the chestnuts lie along the upper terrace like a shining carpet – reflecting light and colour – extraordinary glowing effect. I've never seen it quite so achieved – almost a flat new carpet of golden flame and yet so living and breathing with their own life – now on the ground. I realize it was this effect of light coming through leaves that struck me to the heart the other day as I came up on the top terrace and saw Ruth and the two girls – all somehow bathed in this glowing warm reflected light. I can't bear to think of the leaves being swept up.

NOVEMBER – First icy cold day – felt a paralysing freezing emanation rising from the ground as I walked around.

1966

JANUARY – The first morning when I have revelled in the garden – birds singing, church bells ringing, bulbs springing up everywhere. After such blistering cold and endless days of rain to go out this morning without even a jacket on was like jumping off into the glorious tide of Spring . . .
Aconites just coming – those on soil do better than those in grass. Crocus – heaving up of large Dutch crocus (under oak by Summer House) so powerful that it could be mistaken for moles or some other underground workers – great volcanic breaking of surface.
Extraordinary power of these bulbs. How do they force themselves up in this way?

APRIL – Blistering cold east wind – snow on moor – floods along rivers. Never have I seen Dart like this – brown – thick

Left: the result of work conducted in April 1961 when 20 volunteers, directed by Leeds University lecturer Colin Platt, dug up the lawn in the Private Garden to excavate and fix the date of the Hall's so-called south courtyard. Leonard Elmhirst took part in the dig; Dorothy is said to have wished the spring flowers had been left undisturbed.

– smoothly covering the land. Terrible days for garden. Coldest mid-April on record, save one year. Wet and cold. And yet lovely things are to be seen.

MAY – One of those breathlessly beautiful Sunday mornings when the whole world seems at peace . . . Some collusion somewhere in the universe for this timing. East wind has brought clarity and the sky is an Italian or American deep blue.
Sitting in the Loggia I was quite overcome by the brilliant lime green of the great beech – with the grey of the Ilex and the soft dark velvet green of the yew. Looking in the other direction towards the Circle, the incredible yellow of the rock garden oak makes a marvellous composition with the maroon of *[Prunus] Pissardii* in front. In the evening from the study the late sun shines through the Lucombe and the tulip tree giving a shimmering effect of light.
I stood for a moment under young copper beech on upper drive and felt dazzled by brilliance of crimson leaves against deep blue sky. The colour at the centre is almost orange leading out to startling red at tips.

NOVEMBER – First morning when everything shines and sparkles and golden is our world. Best golds are tulip trees and beeches . . .
Watching leaves twinkling down from top of planes, as they fall, I marvel at their self-directed sense. How do they contrive to find the gaps through which they fall without ever having to halt on the way down? The most extraordinary response to gravitation – faultless, like the perfect movement in a dance. They seem to avoid all the possible obstructions.
. . . We are being given a special

dispensation of beauty this year – with the clear light of north wind and blue sky – which in early morning throws golden glow on the whole scene. Breakfast in my bedroom becomes a sparkling event and Jerry loves so much these highlights of the autumn trees. From my window we gaze across to the upper left corner of Heath Bank – with glorious soft yellow-apricot cherries and strong yellow above

of hedge maple – such a fine composition given by dark yew in front of the warm golden corner. Tulip trees still glorious from my window. The incredible experience is to walk on the upper drive which is entirely covered by orange beech leaves – too much glory. Liquidambar now at its best – so strange to find darkest leaves at the top and some of the palest down at the bottom. The gradation is extraordinary.
Gales last night. Top of younger Lebanon broken off.

1967 *MARCH* –

. . . Disastrous frost suddenly struck us – 12 degrees – and poor *soulangiana* never reached her glory – now brown. We see her from our bedrooms. Other Magnolias cruelly changed and blighted.

APRIL – Despite catastrophe to Magnolias – cherries are superb – the *Spontaneas* in Circle heavenly soft pink and Ukon in Dell has assumed a new importance and glory – and beside our poor mutilated *soulangiana* an arm of beauty is lifted upwards in the rising form of *[Prunus] Temari*. What a spiritual experience is here. The dying back of the one and the resurrection of the other. My heart stopped beating in awe as I realized the meaning of these two – beside one another – death and life bound together – and life filling all the space around.

JULY – Can't believe that such days can continue. Is it east wind that brings this clarity and warm sun and luminous evenings? Last night I walked up over the hill above High Cross and watched sunset over the blue moor hills – then along Broadlears Walk and to my temple – to offer praise and thanksgiving. I felt too happy – too highly favoured. I came home in a state of ecstasy – touching Eleagnus with blessing as I passed.

NOVEMBER – Rushton drove me in car – with chains – up Valley Field so I could sit and contemplate.

Agreed to:

1. Move two *Parrotia* to lower end of field.
2. Take out *Cotoneaster hupehensis*.
3. Add Fothergillas in front of higher plants.
4. Add group Tai Hakus lower down.
5. Two red Acers to be moved out of Heath Bank to open space at bottom where [Mag.] *Lennii* had been.

A still day – cold but sunny – in the stillness the leaves of the beeches were fluttering down – like a game I used to play with Jane trying to catch these

evasive leaves as they fell – runaway leaves always evading capture because so light, so effervescent, so deceptive in their direction and quickness of descent – always a move ahead of my poor heaviness and slow wit to move and grasp – outwitted. *Sorbus hupehensis* – glorious pink berries.

DECEMBER – Flora – approach from top steps disconcerting because we see William's hut above the yews and the view beyond is so mixed and so thin that the eye finds no comfort – restless – spotty – must plant something high and thick.

1968

MARCH – Sunday morning with Jerry in the garden – the first time I have been able to go out and enjoy what I see. For weeks now we have been under the blight of east wind that can darken our days and spread gloom. Strange it is – the effect of these depressing days from the east. And now suddenly today the wind has changed into the north bringing sun and strong blue sky, and hopefulness back into the heart. Terry says at least the weather has been dry – enabling us to do a lot of work – such as dealing with the drain at the foot of the Heath Bank – and turfing the left corner where the old *Mag. Lennei* has been removed and two Acers planted.
... One of the perfect days full of stillness and sunshine. Ecstasy swept over me as I heard my first blackbird singing.

APRIL – A pleasant day for Mr Cane's visit. The slope with white star-like daffodils at its best and the Magnolias glorious and Tai Hakus at their peak. He was delighted with Eldorado and with the angle of Flora. Worked on Flora's corner – he says we must dig out lower part of the yellow-green *Cupressus* – leaving the top and fill in with yew. A curved bench (not as long as semi-circular) can be placed on the corner. Pieris to be removed – replace with some darker evergreen.

Later in the morning he placed canes to mark the new line for outer side of Glade. While around Flora he cut out, from the plans he had brought, the exact size of the stone balls to be placed on the old heavy pillars. Such an endearing proceeding – Mr Cane sitting at foot of steps by Flora using Jerry's scissors to cut around, from his thick drawing paper, the exact form of the two balls.

SEPTEMBER – Coming back after 3 weeks at Chalet I am struck by the growth – the tremendous growth of everything – all the shrubs and trees look gloriously full of life and rich in development. I've never felt it so strongly before and never have I been so conscious of the perfect shape of it all. The form is so clear, so strong – so exciting in every part of the garden – what a revelation is here – of beauty, of variety, of interest that never ceases to draw me deeper into the mystery of this wonderful place. And this is a time of few flowers.

NOVEMBER – Autumn colours. Not a good year – but the oaks and elms give gold effect and the tulip trees are marvellous. After warm October and warmer early November – we are now in the cold blast of east winds.
... Lovely views of golden colour on every side – so warm and glowing. From my bedroom the shades of yellow and apricot and orange give the most

welcoming warm lighting-up of the landscape and all the various tones of yellow compensate for the lack of reds.

Courtyard:
1. *Camellia sasanqua* full of flower – so brave, so vulnerable, so terribly touching.
2. *Jasminum nudiflorum* full out on Barn Theatre wall. Emily brought it into my bedroom – so amazing how the flower shoots out fully open from the bare stem.

Dorothy Elmhirst died on 14 December 1968, a few weeks before her eighty-second birthday.

A Apostles
B Beech
C Cedars
Dav. Davidia
Deo. Deodar
E Eleagnus umbellata
G Ginko Biloba
I Ilex (Holm oak)
Ley. Leyland cypress
Lib. Libocedrus
Liqu. Liquidambar
L.O. Lucombe Oak
L.P. London plane
M.H. Malus hupehensis
M.P. Monterey pine
S.C. Spanish chestnuts
S.P. Scots pines
T.D. Taxodium distichum
T.H. Tai Haku
T.O. Turkey oak
Y Prunus yedoensis

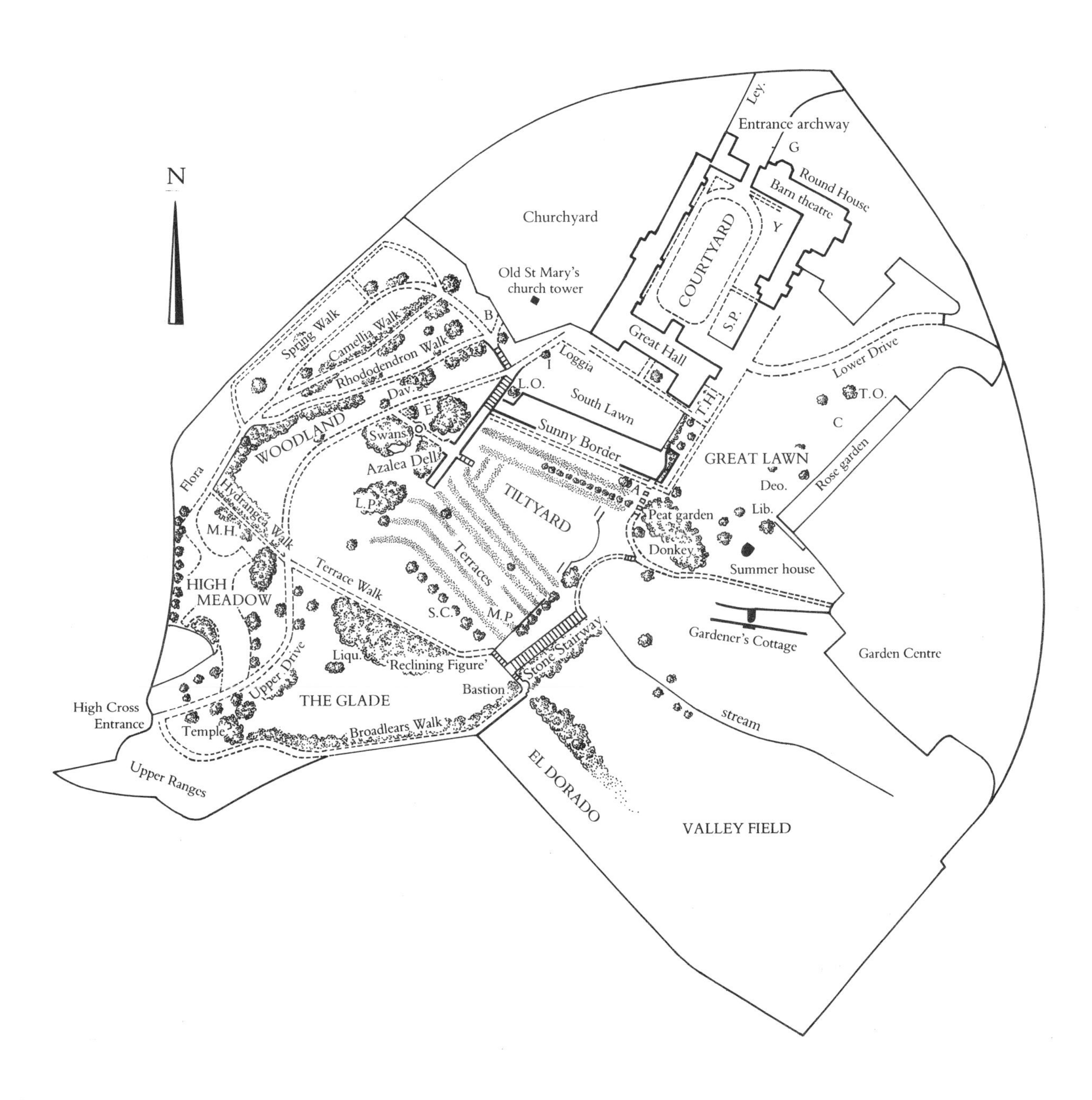
N
Ley.
Entrance archway
G
Round House
Barn theatre
Y
Churchyard
Old St Mary's
church tower
COURTYARD
S.P.
Great Hall
Loggia
I
L.O.
South Lawn
T.H.
Lower Drive
T.O.
C
Spring Walk
Camellia Walk
Rhododendron Walk
B
Dav.
E
WOODLAND
Swans
Azalea Dell
Sunny Border
GREAT LAWN
Rose garden
Deo.
Lib.
A
Flora
Hydrangea Walk
L.P.
TILTYARD
Peat garden
Donkey
Summer house
M.H.
HIGH
MEADOW
Terrace Walk
Terraces
S.C.
M.P.
Gardener's Cottage
Garden Centre
Upper Drive
Liqu.
'Reclining Figure'
Stone Stairway
Bastion
High Cross
Entrance
THE GLADE
Temple
Broadlears Walk
stream
Upper Ranges
EL DORADO
VALLEY FIELD

The publishers wish to thank the following for providing photographs reproduced in this book.

Chaplin Jones: pp. 20, 21, 33, 40, 51 (right), 53, 77, 80, 85, 86 (right), 87 (right), 91, 93.
Kate Mount: pp. 35, 39, 42, 43, 46, 47, 54, 55, 58, 59, 61, 63 (right), 66, 67, 70, 74, 78 (left), 79 (right), 81, 87 (centre), 92 (right).
James Ravilious: p. 13.
Dumbarton Oaks (Trustees for Harvard University): p.34.
Openeye Photo Agency and Library: pp. 38, 51 (left), 63 (left).
Iris Hardwick: p.26

Other photographs, the majority taken by Leonard Elmhirst, are reproduced with the kind permission of the Dartington Hall Trust Records Office.